THE NON-DRINKER'S DRINK BOOK

THE
NON-DRINKER'S
DRINK BOOK

Betty Rollin

*

Recipes by Lucy Rosenfeld

*

Drawings by Sergio Aragonés

GARDEN CITY, NEW YORK

Doubleday & Company, Inc.

1966

FOR THEIR KIND HELP, WE WISH TO THANK

Alcoholics Anonymous; B. Altman & Co.; Bloomingdale's; Campbell Soup Co.; Miss Elizabeth Carpenter, Press Secretary to Mrs. Lyndon B. Johnson; H. A. Cassebeer Pharmacy; Celebration Specialties, Ltd.; The Coca-Cola Co.; Coffee Brewing Institute; Cott Beverage Corp.; Dannon Milk Products, Inc.; The Frederick Lewis Allen Room; Hamilton-Beach Co.; Hoffman Beverage Co.; Holland House Brands, Inc.; Meier's Wine Cellars, Inc.; Minute Maid Co.; Varco, Inc. (Moulinex); National Dairy Council; The Nestle Company, Inc.; Kirsch Beverages, Inc.; Ocean Spray Cranberries, Inc.; John Oster Manufacturing Co.; Pepsi-Cola Co.; Mrs. George W. Romney; Sands Hotel, Las Vegas, Nevada; Sardi's Restaurant; Schrafft's; Schweppes (U.S.A.) Ltd.; Sealtest Foods; Spice Club Foods, Inc.; Sunbeam Corporation; Sunkist Growers, Inc.; Tea Council of the U.S.A., Inc.; Waring Products Corp.

CONTENTS

INTRODUCTION	9
EQUIPMENT THAT CAN ONLY HELP	11
DEFINITIONS AND EXPLANATIONS	15
COCKTAILS: ZERO PROOF	17
What To Do with Ginger Ale, Besides Pour It	19
The Other Standards	29
The Juices: Fruit and Vegetable	37
Extracts, Essences, Etceteras	69
Bogus Booze	79
Punch	91
DRINKS FOR AFTER DINNER AND LONG BEFORE	103
Coffee	105
Tea	119
(Other) Hot Shots	131
Mostly Milk	143
From the Fountain (Yours)	161

CHARTS AND TABLES 181

    Herbs and Garnishes 183

    Weights and Measures 189

    Equivalents 191

    Yields 193

    Calorie Chart 195

INDEX 201

Introduction

Non-drinkers of the world, you needn't unite (what a bore if you did—can you image a malted convention?) but do stop slinking about at cocktail parties swallowing ginger ale and Coca-Cola, as if such liquid punishment were, not only all there is, but what you deserve.

I am not suggesting that at parties you bring your own carrot juice. Nor should you show up anywhere at 5:30 with an electric blender under your arm ("A martini? Har, har, not for me, Marge! Just give me some of that pot roast left over from last night's dinner, a squirt or two of soda water, and—"), no.

Similarly, if, after explaining that you don't drink, your host regards you as if you were an Untouchable and pulls his shoulder out reaching behind the sink for a warm Coke that has been there since last August, there is nothing to do but add ice and look grateful. His education must begin at home, but not at his—yours.

The burden (or pleasure) of change lies squarely on the host—and on the hostess, even if her only guest is a non-drinking husband. It takes a woman to say, "Here's a gin and tonic without the gin, darling," and make it work, let alone make it.* A woman can most easily attach non-drinker's drink ideas to an already fluent cooking vocabulary. Everyone is a "non-drinker" *some* of the time. Even near-alcoholics want a glass of orange juice once in a while. (Why not make

* A friend's husband, getting overly in the spirit of things, snapped at his wife, "This is *not* a gin and tonic without gin; it's a *vodka* and tonic without *vodka!*"

it peach nectar instead?! Just add some pineapple juice, a little dried tarragon, and—oh, never mind.) The point is, simply, to make the small effort it takes for a non-alcoholic drink to taste good, to have some originality, to look pretty, if that is important—or to look like a "real drink," if *that* is important.

Because of health, religion, age, weight, money, or simple dislike, almost one-fourth of the nation's adult population, plus all children (we hope), are out there not-drinking. Here are three hundred and fifty-one things to do about it.

Equipment That Can Only Help

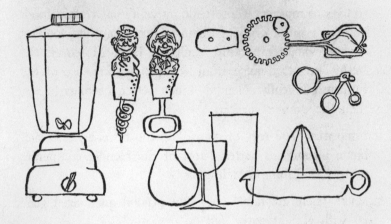

ELECTRIC BLENDER: It is foolish, I know, to lose heartbeats over a kitchen appliance, but the unalloyed joy of owning an electric blender is enough to make grown non-drinkers cry. The blender chops, grates, aerates, whips, and blends. It makes drinks out of food. It makes froth out of liquid calm. It makes something unheard of out of something heard of too often. Get one, friends, get one! And if you do, hear this:

1. It is a good idea, usually, to start the blender on "Low."
2. Cut solids into one-inch pieces.
3. Do not crush ice in the blender, unless you add one small cube at a time to at least two cups of liquid.
4. Blenders do not whip egg whites; nor do they extract juices from fruits or vegetables.

ELECTRIC JUICE EXTRACTOR: It is possible, I hear, to muddle through life without a juice extractor, and it does make a terrible commotion. Still, since the extractor extracts (by centrifugal force) the natural vitamin- and mineral-filled juices from fruits and vegetables, the juicer is a great boon to lives of mothers whose children won't eat certain foods but don't mind drinking them—a good solution, too, for anyone who, temporarily, can't eat bulk. Moreover, the freshly extracted juice from almost anything, except the furniture, is really splendid—much better, needless to say, than the canned versions.

ICE CRUSHER: You can, of course, do the towel-hammer act, but a machine is better. Most of the blender companies make ice-crushing attachments.

SHAKER: There are fancy ones, but a good quart-sized glass jar with a tight cover will do.

ORANGE JUICE SQUEEZER

ICE BUCKET

ROTARY (EGG) BEATER: electric or manual

CAN AND BOTTLE OPENERS

STRAINER

ENAMEL SAUCEPAN

DOUBLE BOILER

MEASURING CUPS AND SPOONS

RUBBER SPATULA: This is helpful if a vortex forms when you are using an electric blender.

BOTTLE CAPS OR CORKS

PITCHER

PUNCH BOWL

GLASSES OF EVERY KIND: The essential ones are highball and cocktail.

GLASS HOLDERS FOR HOT DRINKS

CUPS: Coffee, tea, demitasse, mugs, punch

COFFEE POTS: drip, percolator, or vacuum, and espresso

TEAPOT: earthenware recommended

STRAWS

TOOTHPICKS (for garnishes)

SPOONS: tall and short

Definitions and Explanations

A "Non-Drinker's Drink" is a non-alcoholic drink. A non-alcoholic drink, according to the code of Federal Regulations, is any product with less than one-half of 1% alcohol.

Drinks in this book are categorized according to their most distinctive characteristics. Where the matter is debatable, notes after recipes and at the end of chapters indicate the whereabouts of the drinks in question.

Accompanying food is suggested at random.

(B) means the use of a blender is necessary. When the use of a blender is only suggested, it says so in the recipe.

(D) means the drink is especially dietetic. The section on skim milk abounds with diet drinks. However, most other recipes in the book can be transformed into low-calorie drinks by making the usual substitutions, i.e., dietetic syrups and sodas for the other kind; skim milk for whole milk; saccharin for sugar, etc.

(JE) means the use of a juice extractor is necessary.

"Blend" means blend with an electric blender.

"Beat" means beat with a manual or electric egg beater, unless otherwise stated.

"Shake" means shake in a cocktail shaker.

"Glass" means an eight-ounce highball glass.

"Tall glass" means a ten-ounce collins glass.

"Very tall glass" means a taller-than-ten-ounce collins glass.

"Soda glass" means a twelve- or fourteen-ounce glass.

"Juice glass" and "small glass" mean a four- to six-ounce glass.

"Cup" means an eight-ounce cup.

"Punch cup" means a four-ounce cup.

When you make cold drinks, it is generally a good idea to pre-chill the glasses.

Crushed ice blended with a drink makes it frothier.

Club soda and carbonated water are, in this book, interchangeable. So are shaved and crushed ice. So are the words "thawed" and "defrosted." "Snow" is finely crushed ice, not packed tightly.

COCKTAILS:
ZERO PROOF

What To Do with Ginger Ale, Besides Pour It

Ginger ale isn't all bad. It just needs help. When it is not used alone, but as a major ingredient, ginger ale has several noteworthy advantages: (1) It is usually there, as opposed to, for instance, the rose-flower water needed in ROSE AFSHOREH (in a later chapter); (2) It takes very little to make ginger ale better—a few squirts of fruit juice will do it (they are also usually there); (3) Ginger Ale Plus is just the thing for *beginning* non-drink drinkers—sort of like trying London before Iraq; and (4) unless you add grape juice, ice cream, or cerise food coloring, ginger ale drinks look like The Other Kind.

GINGER ALE AND JUICE

I

Juice of ½ lemon   *Ginger ale*
1 teaspoon sugar   *Slice of lemon*
½ cup cracked ice

Shake together lemon juice, sugar, and cracked ice. Pour into 1 tall glass. Fill with ginger ale. Garnish with lemon slice.

GINGER ALE AND JUICE

II

Juice of ½ lime   *Ginger ale*
½ cup cracked ice   *Maraschino cherry*

Shake together lime juice and cracked ice. Add ginger ale. Serve in 1 tall glass. Garnish with cherry.

GINGER ALE AND JUICE

III

1 ounce fresh lemon juice   *Ice cubes*
3 ounces grape juice   *Ginger ale*

Pour juices over ice cubes in 1 tall glass. Fill with ginger ale.

GINGER ALE AND JUICE

IV

1 ounce cranberry juice   Ice cubes
1 ounce fresh orange juice   Ginger ale

Pour juices over ice cubes in 1 tall glass. Fill with ginger ale.

GINGER ALE AND JUICE

V

2 ounces fresh orange juice   2 ounces grape juice
2 ounces canned pineapple   Ice cubes
    juice   Ginger ale

Pour juices over ice cubes in 2 tall glasses. Fill with ginger ale.

SHIRLEY TEMPLE SARDI

Served to children at Sardi's Restaurant in New York in lieu of a champagne cocktail—trappings intact.

Dash grenadine   Maraschino cherry
Crushed ice
Ginger ale (served in ice
    bucket)

Pour grenadine over crushed ice in 1 champagne glass. Fill with ginger ale. Garnish with cherry. Serve with muddler.

PONY'S NECK

1 lemon
⅓ cup grapefruit juice
Sugar to taste

½ cup cracked ice
Ginger ale

Peel lemon in long spiral. Squeeze juice from peeled lemon. Place peel in tall glass, letting some hang over the top. Pour lemon juice, grapefruit juice, and sugar into shaker with cracked ice. Shake and pour into glass with peel. Fill with ginger ale.

CIDER RICKEY

2 ounces orange juice
3 ounces sweet cider
Cracked ice

Ginger ale
1 strip cucumber rind

Shake together orange juice, cider, and cracked ice. Strain. Pour into 1 tall, cold glass. Fill with ginger ale. Garnish with cucumber rind.

LEMON FROTH

¾ glass (6 ounces) ginger ale
1 tablespoon lemon-and-lime syrup

1 tablespoon cracked ice
Beaten egg white
Slice of lemon
Maraschino cherry

Shake together ginger ale, syrup, and ice. Strain into 1 tall glass. Stir in egg white. Garnish with lemon slice and cherry.

GINGERPARILLA

Ginger ale   Thin slice of lemon rind
1 tablespoon sarsaparilla   Cracked ice
  syrup   Sprig of mint

Stir all ingredients except mint in 1 tall glass. Garnish with fresh mint.

WHITE GRAPE NECTAR

½ cup muscat grape juice   Ice cubes
  (white)   Ginger ale
Juice of 1 lemon   2 slices lime
1 egg white

Shake together grape juice, lemon juice, and egg white. Pour over ice cubes in 2 tall glasses. Fill with ginger ale. Garnish with lime.

GINGER FROTH

Juice of ½ fresh lime   Ginger ale
Juice of ½ fresh lemon   ½ teaspoon grated lime
½ teaspoon grenadine   rind
1 egg white   Thin finger of fresh
Ice cubes   pineapple

Shake together juices, grenadine, egg white, and ice cubes. Pour into 1 tall glass. Fill with ginger ale. Sprinkle grated rind on top. Add pineapple.

TALL CLOVE PURPLE

I

⅔ glass ginger ale
⅓ cup grape juice
Dash powdered clove

Shaved ice
Slice of orange
Several whole cloves

Stir together ginger ale, grape juice, and powdered clove. Strain. Pour over shaved ice in 1 tall glass. Garnish with orange slice stuck with whole cloves.

TALL CLOVE PURPLE

II

⅔ glass ginger ale
½ teaspoon blackberry
  syrup
Dash powdered clove

Shaved ice
Slice of orange
Several whole cloves

Stir together ginger ale, blackberry syrup, and powdered clove. Strain. Pour over shaved ice in 1 tall glass. Garnish with orange slice stuck with whole cloves.

PROHIBITION SPICE

3 slices orange strips
Several drops lemon juice
1 glass ginger ale

4 tablespoons cracked ice
Powdered dry ginger

Add orange strips and lemon juice to ½ glass ginger ale. Refrigerate several hours. Serve in 1 tall glass with cracked ice. Add rest of ginger ale to fill glass. Sprinkle powdered ginger on top.

MINT MIST

2 egg whites
⅓ cup mint jelly
Juice of 1 lemon

1½ cups ginger ale (12-ounce bottles)

Beat egg whites until stiff, but not dry. Add mint jelly and lemon juice. Continue beating until jelly is dissolved and egg whites are pale green. Slowly pour and fold in the ginger ale. Transfer to 2 freezing trays. Place in freezer. When frozen to a snow-soft consistency, remove to a chilled bowl. Beat until smooth. Serve in cocktail glasses with small spoons. Serves 4.

CARIBBEAN COCKTAIL (B)

1 chilled papaya
2 glasses ginger ale
   (1-pint bottle)

Crushed ice
4 slices lime

Peel and seed papaya. Add to 1 cup of the ginger ale and blend on high speed until ingredients are creamy and liquefied. Pour over crushed ice in 4 cocktail glasses. Add remaining ginger ale to fill glasses. Stir gently. Decorate rims of glasses with lime slices.

HERB SIZZLE

1 tablespoon dried
   rosemary leaves
1 teaspoon sugar
Pinch salt
¼ cup water
1 tablespoon lemon juice

¾ cup chilled pear nectar
1½ glasses chilled ginger
   ale (12-ounce bottle)
Crushed ice
4 slices lemon

Simmer rosemary leaves, sugar, salt, and water for 3 minutes. Cool. Strain. Discard leaves. Add lemon juice, pear nectar and ginger ale to liquid. Stir once. Pour over ice in 4 tall glasses. Garnish with lemon slices.

MIXED FRUIT THAW

1 ten-ounce package frozen mixed fruit, thawed
Ice cubes
1 quart ginger ale

Distribute fruit over ice cubes in 4 tall glasses. Fill with ginger ale. Stir.

PEACH THAW

1 ten-ounce package frozen
  sliced peaches, thawed
2 tablespoons lemon juice
⅔ cup sugar
¼ teaspoon ground nutmeg

¼ teaspoon ground ginger
1 one-pint-twelve-ounce
  bottle ginger ale, chilled
4 slices naval orange

Combine peaches, lemon juice, sugar, nutmeg, and ginger. Mash together thoroughly or blend in an electric blender. Put equal amounts into 4 tall, cold glasses (10-ounce). Add ginger ale. Put thin slice of orange into each glass. Serves 4.

The Other Standards

Like ginger ale, The Other Standards (tonics, club sodas, and colas) have the availability/familiarity virtue.

The most successful stand-by-itself Standard is Bitter Lemon*, the black tie of non-alcoholic straight-from-the-bottle drinks. It is advertised by Schweppes, in their enchantingly snooty way, as "the only soft drink children don't like." Speaking of things being good right out of the bottle, the cocktail mixes aren't, but with club soda they're fine—tart and lemon-y, not unlike Bitter Lemon straight.

* The ingredients are, mostly, fresh lemons and tonic.

TONIC DRINK

I

Tonic
Ice cubes
Slice of unpeeled cucumber

Pour tonic over cubes in 1 glass. Add cucumber slice.

TONIC DRINK

II

1½ ounces orange (or lemon or lime) juice
Shaved ice
Tonic

Pour juice over ice in 1 glass. Fill with tonic.

COFFEE TONIC

½ cup iced coffee   *Ice cubes*
Sugar syrup to taste*   *½ cup tonic*

Pour coffee and syrup over cubes in 1 glass. Fill with tonic.

*SIMPLE SUGAR SYRUP

1 cup sugar
1 cup water

Boil together for about 3 minutes. Can be refrigerated in tightly covered jar.

TEA TONIC

½ cup iced tea   Ice cubes
Sugar syrup to taste   ½ cup tonic

Pour tea and syrup over cubes in 1 glass. Fill with tonic.

BITTER LEMON

I

Bitter Lemon   Cracked ice
Several dashes Angostura   Twist of lemon peel
   bitters

Combine all ingredients, except lemon peel, in 1 tall, cold glass. Garnish with lemon peel.

BITTER LEMON

II

Pale pink, and slightly sweeter than the others.

Bitter Lemon
1 tablespoon grenadine (or to taste if sweeter drink is
   preferred)
Shaved ice

Combine in 1 tall, cold glass.

BITTER LEMON

III

Equal parts:
  Bitter Lemon
  Cranberry juice
  Cracked ice

Combine in 1 tall, cold glass.

BITTER LEMON

IV

Bitter Lemon	*Cracked ice*
2 tablespoons mint syrup	*Fresh sprig of mint*

Combine all ingredients, except mint sprig, in 1 tall, cold glass. Garnish with mint.

BITTER LEMON

V

5 small bottles Bitter	*½ cup water*
Lemon or lemon soda	*3 tablespoons lime juice*
½ cup mint jelly	*8 slices lime*

Fill ice cube trays with 2 bottles of soda or Bitter Lemon. Freeze. Refrigerate remaining bottles. Heat mint jelly and water to make syrup. Cool. Add lime juice. Shave or crack lemon ice cubes and place in 8 tall glasses. Add 3 tablespoons of the syrup to each glass. Fill with chilled Bitter Lemon or lemon soda. Garnish with lime slices.

Note: Other Bitter Lemon drinks are in the fruit juice and punch sections.

PINK DRINK

3 teaspoons grenadine   Club soda
Shaved ice   Twist of lemon peel
Dash Angostura bitters

Pour grenadine over shaved ice into a cocktail glass. Add dash of bitters. Fill glass with club soda. Garnish with lemon peel.

CALCUTTA COLA

This seems unlikely, but it works.

Chopped ice   Several drops fresh lime
2 tablespoons canned,   juice
    crushed pineapple   Chilled cola
    Curry powder

Half fill 1 tall glass with ice. Add crushed pineapple and lime juice. Pour cola over all. Stir briefly. Sprinkle curry powder on top.

MINT COLA

1 teaspoon lemon juice	Ice cubes
⅛ teaspoon peppermint extract	Slice of lemon
Cola	Mint candy stick

Pour lemon juice, extract, and cola over ice cubes in 1 tall glass. Garnish with lemon slice. Use mint candy stick as muddler.

LEMON-EGG COLA

1 egg	2 tablespoons lemon juice
Chopped ice	Grated nutmeg
Cola	

Beat egg until lemon-yellow and frothy. Half fill 4 tall glasses with chopped ice. Put ¼ of beaten egg into each glass. Add cola and lemon juice. Stir briefly. Sprinkle grated nutmeg over top of each glass. Serve immediately.

Note: Other colas in *From the Fountain (Yours)*.

CONEY ISLAND ROOT BEER

1 twelve-ounce bottle root beer	½ lime
Ice cubes	Curl of lime rind

Pour root beer over ice cubes. Squeeze ¼ fresh lime into each of 2 tall glasses. Decorate with lime rind.

SEVENTEEN

½ cup minted apple jelly
3 twelve-ounce bottles chilled root beer
¼ cup lemon juice

Break up jelly with fork. Mix with 1 bottle root beer and 1 tablespoon lemon juice. Pour into an ice cube tray and freeze. (Mixture will not become as firm as ice.) Remove from ice tray and divide into 5 tall glasses. Add remaining lemon juice and root beer. Stir once. Served with iced tea spoons.

The Juices: Fruit and Vegetable

Juice, in case your mother never told you, is "the liquid part of a plant, fruit, or vegetable." (The definition goes on, but we needn't.) Juice, the point is, carries with it a strong food identity, and strong identities must be combined with care or, in the words of no great scholar I ever knew, they taste terrible.

I will not go into the healthful routine about juice. Everyone knows that juice is healthful. Americans practically everywhere down orange juice every morning with unerring regularity; and, in the event of a virus or flu, juice, as Nature's Own Medicine, is administered more frequently than aspirin. All the while, overlooked as the Beautiful Secretary in the Wrong Clothes (it was never her glasses), are the pleasures of juice: it mixes well, it is surprisingly varied (parsnips *do* have juice, Virginia), it is bracing and delicious in its special clean-cool way, and all tolled, fruit juice remains the best thirst-quencher of the non-boozes—or of the boozes, for that matter.

Scotch-on-the-rocks is no cure for dehydration, and it's hard to swallow those little ginger ale bubbles very fast. Water is all right for thirst, of course, but it's boring.

Juice is best at dinner parties where, as a before-dinner drink, it starts the dinner instead of finishing it. I have lost count of The Dinner Parties I Have Known where, through drinking, the guests lost all taste-consciousness. Pity the hostess who, after toiling all day over squash surprise, watches her guests mistake it for succotash.

Juices may be served in order to virtually connect with the dinner that follows. JUICE JULEP, for instance, in the fruit juice section, "connects" with lamb, FARM FROTH in *Vegetable Juices* works like a fanfare for English Dover sole. It is a question, rather than having a drink before dinner, of starting dinner with a drink. You decide.

ADES

An ade—"a sweetened drink made of water and fruit juice"— is the best-known simple fruit juice drink. Much of the time it is terrible. It needn't be.

LEMONADE (BASIC)

Cracked ice   *Soda or water*
Juice of 1 lemon   *Mint*
1 tablespoon sugar syrup or
* 2 teaspoons powdered*
* sugar*

Partly fill 1 tall glass with cracked ice. Add lemon juice, syrup, then soda (or water). Additional syrup may be used for sweeter drink. Garnish with mint.

OTHER ADES

Follow basic lemonade recipe using the following instead of lemon juice:

Juices of 1 lime and ½
* lemon*
*   or*
Juices of 1 lime and 1
* orange*
*   or*

Juices of 1 lemon and 1
* orange*
*   or*
Juices of 4 kumquats
* (JE) and 1 lime*

PINK LEMONADE

Cracked ice
Juice of 1 lemon
1 tablespoon raspberry
* syrup or grenadine*

Soda or water
Maraschino cherry

Partly fill 1 tall glass with cracked ice. Add lemon juice, syrup (or grenadine), then soda (or water). Garnish with cherry.

GOLDEN LEMONADE

Juice of 1 lemon
2 teaspoons powered
* sugar*
1 egg yolk

6 ounces water or soda
Crushed ice
Slice of orange
Maraschino cherry

Shake all ingredients except orange slice and cherry. Strain into 1 very tall glass. Garnish with the orange slice and cherry.

AGUA DE MELAO

Juice of 1 lemon   Molasses
1 glass water   Ice cubes

Add juice to water. Sweeten to taste with molasses. Serve very cold in 2 small glasses filled with ice cubes.

SPICED LEMONADE

1 quart basic lemonade   1 teaspoon allspice
  (using 4 or 5 lemons   4 cloves
  and 1 quart water,   Ice cubes
  sweetened to taste)   4 slices lemon, stuck with
2 cups water   cloves
1 small piece cinnamon   Grated nutmeg

Boil water with spices. Simmer about 8 minutes. Strain. Chill. Add to lemonade. Cool. Pour over ice cubes in 4 tall glasses. Garnish with lemon slices. Sprinkle grated nutmeg over each drink.

FRUIT JUICE

INSTANT WAIKIKI

½ small can pineapple   ⅛ teaspoon brown sugar
  juice   Crushed ice
Juice of ½ lemon

Shake all ingredients, and fill 1 tall glass.

MORNING COCKTAIL

Juice of 1 orange   1 teaspoon egg white
1 teaspoon grenadine   ½ cup cracked ice

Shake all ingredients vigorously. Strain. Serve in 1 cocktail glass.

GIN-LESS GIMLET

Juice of ½ lime   2 teaspoons sugar syrup
1 egg white   (or to taste)
2 dashes Angostura bitters   Ice cubes

Shake all ingredients vigorously. Strain into 1 cocktail glass.

CHERRY PINK

Juice of 1 large navel   Small amount egg white
  orange   Shaved ice
1 tablespoon cherry syrup   Slice of orange
1 teaspoon spiced sugar
  syrup*

Shake all ingredients except slice of orange. Pour into 1 sour glass. Serve very cold with orange slice on rim of glass.

*SPICED SUGAR SYRUP

4 whole cloves   3 slices unpeeled navel
⅓ cup water   orange
1 cup sugar
2 or 3 slices unpeeled
lemon

Tie cloves tightly in cheesecloth bag. Place in saucepan with
water, sugar, lemon, and orange. Boil 5 minutes. Remove
cheesecloth bag. Yields 1 cup syrup.

PALM BEACH COCKTAIL

Juice of 1 orange   1 egg yolk
Juice of ½ lemon   1 tablespoon mint syrup
1 teaspoon grenadine   Cracked ice

Shake all ingredients and pour into 2 cocktail glasses.

1920 COCKTAIL

1 tablespoon lime juice   Cracked ice
⅓ cup grape juice
1 teaspoon egg white, or
several drops egg white
substitute

Shake all ingredients and pour into 1 cocktail glass.

LAVENDER-LEMON HIGHBALL

1½ cups grape juice   Powdered sugar to taste
1½ cups lemon juice   Crushed ice
1 egg   Soda

Shake all ingredients except soda. Strain. Add soda to fill.
Serve in 4 tall glasses.

HONEY GRAPE DRINK

⅔ cup grape juice   1 egg white
1 tablespoon honey   Ice cubes
Juice of 1 lime   Club soda

Combine grape juice, honey, and lime juice in a bowl. Beat
egg white until stiff, but not dry. Add beaten egg white, a
small amount at a time, to fruit juices, beating well with a
wire whisk after each addition. Pour over ice cubes into 2 tall
glasses (10-ounce). Fill glasses with soda. Garnish with swirl
of lime peel. Serves 2.

FRUIT BOWL (B)

1 cup sweetened grapefruit   ½ banana
   juice   Powdered clove
½ cup pear nectar   Ice cubes
Juice of 1 lime

Blend together juices, banana, and clove. Pour over ice in 2
tall glasses.

BANANA FOAM (B)

1 banana
½ cup grape juice
2 strips lemon rind, cut
    small

2 strips orange rind, cut
    small
Cracked ice
1 beaten egg white

Blend all ingredients except egg white. Fill 2 tall glasses. Add beaten egg white to each glass. Stir once.

PINK SANDS

Served at the bar of the Sands Hotel in Las Vegas, Nevada.

1 small can pineapple
    juice
½ teaspoon sugar

2 tablespoons cream
Dash grenadine
Cracked ice

Pour all ingredients over cracked ice in 1 tall glass. Stir.

PINEAPPLE FROTH

1 teaspoon dried marjoram
⅓ cup water
1 cup chilled pineapple
    juice

Part of egg white
Ice cubes

Simmer marjoram in water for about 5 minutes. Cool. Strain and discard leaves. Shake with other ingredients until frothy. Discard ice cubes. Serve immediately in 1 tall glass.

LEMONESCENCE

¼ teaspoon dried
   tarragon leaves
¼ cup hot water
⅓ cup peach nectar

⅓ cup pineapple juice
Ice cubes
Bottled bitter lemon

Simmer tarragon in water for 2 to 3 minutes. Cool. Strain. Mix liquid with juices. Pour over ice cubes in 1 tall glass (10-ounce). Fill with bitter lemon. Stir briefly. Serves 1.

PINEAPPLE MINT

2 cups pineapple juice
Ice cubes
2 drops mint extract

1 cup chilled Bitter
   Lemon

Pour juice over ice cubes in 3 tall glasses. Add extract, then Bitter Lemon. Stir.

HERBED FRUIT (B)

Juice of 2 oranges (1 cup)
½ cup frozen peaches
   (defrosted, but very
   cold)

1 rounded teaspoon dried
   tarragon leaves
Juice of ½ lemon
2 teaspoons honey

Blend all ingredients, first on low speed for several seconds, then on high for about 20 seconds. When drink is rich and foamy, pour into 2 glasses.

PINEAPPLE PINK

2 teaspoons dried   2½ cups pineapple juice
   marjoram leaves   1 cup frozen raspberries
½ cup water

Simmer marjoram leaves and water together until water is
half original amount. Strain. Discard leaves and cool liquid.
Add to pineapple juice. Put raspberries through wire sieve or
into electric blender for several seconds. Add to herb juice.
Serve cold in fruit juice or cocktail glasses. Yields about 3
glasses.

BLENDER "DAIQUIRIS" (B)

LIME "DAIQUIRI" (B)

4 tablespoons frozen   1 cup crushed ice
   limeade concentrate,   3 drops mint extract
   thawed   Maraschino cherry

Blend limeade, ice, and mint extract in blender for a few
seconds on high speed. If vortex is formed, stop motor and
move ingredients from side of glass with a rubber spatula.
Blend again until fine "snow" is formed. Serve in cocktail
glass with short straw. Garnish with cherry. Serves 1.

ORANGE "DAIQUIRI" (B)

2 heaping tablespoons
  frozen orangeade
  concentrate
1 cup shaved ice

1 teaspoon grenadine or
  maraschino juice
Slice of navel orange

Follow directions for LIME "DAIQUIRI." Trim rim of glass with orange slice.

PINEAPPLE "DAIQUIRI" (B)

⅛ cup canned pineapple
1 tablespoon lime juice
1½ teaspoons sugar

½ cup cracked ice
Sprig of mint

Follow directions for LIME "DAIQUIRI." Garnish with mint.

ORANGE FROST

Has a daiquiri consistency.

1 cup frozen orange juice
  concentrate
1 teaspoon lemon juice
1 egg

1 tablespoon sugar
½ cup cracked ice
½ teaspoon grated orange
  rind

Beat or blend all ingredients, except orange rind, until foamy. Serve in 4 cocktail glasses. Top with orange rind.

ISLAND MIST (B)

1 six-ounce can frozen
orange juice concentrate
1 tablespoon confectioners'
sugar
½ cup canned, crushed
pineapple

2 strips lime rind
(cut up)
1 teaspoon almond extract
1 cup cracked ice
5 fresh sprigs mint

Partially thaw orange juice concentrate. Blend all ingredients,
except mint, for about 30 seconds. Serve in 5 cocktail glasses
with short straws. Garnish with sprig of mint.

JUICE JULEP

This is almost (almost, I said) like white wine. The hint of
mint makes it grand with lamb.

About 3 sprigs mint
1 pint white grape juice
Juice of 1 lemon
4 tablespoons grapefruit
juice

1 cup grated pineapple
Pinch salt
Pinch nutmeg
Ice cubes

Bruise mint in a pitcher. Add other ingredients. Stir. Chill.
Strain and pour over ice in 4 tall glasses.

GRAPEFRUIT GINGER (B)

This is a pungent drink, especially with ginger.

4 dried apricot halves
¾ cup cold, unsweetened
  grapefruit juice
1 teaspoon honey

2 tablespoons crushed ice
Powdered ginger
  (optional)

Soak apricots in water until pliable. Cut them up and put in blender container with a little grapefruit juice. Blend for a few seconds. Add remaining juice and honey. Blend again. Serve over crushed ice in 1 tall glass. Sprinkle ginger on top.

MINT APRICOT (B)

¾ cup cold, unsweetened
  grapefruit juice
2 rounded teaspoons
  apricot butter

4 after-dinner mints
Crushed ice

Blend all ingredients together until creamy and very smooth. Serve in 1 tall glass.

PALE CITRON (B)

Thick and delicious. Considering what it looks and tastes like, this is a low-calorie drink.

2 cups orange juice   3 tablespoons lemon juice
½ cup cooked, sweetened   1 cup cracked ice
   dried apricots

Combine all ingredients and blend in an electric blender until smooth and liquid becomes frothy. Serve in 8-ounce glasses. Serves 4.

All of the following drinks, made with apple juice, are good Christmas cocktails, and best followed by poultry, game, or roast pork.

APRICOT APPLE (B)

½ cup dried apricots   1 cup crushed ice
1 cup apple juice   Cinnamon

Soak apricots until pliable. Cut them into small pieces. Blend all ingredients until liquefied. Serve in 2 glasses.

SUMMER APPLE

1 cup sweet cider   ½ piece preserved ginger*
½ cup cherry juice   ½ cup crushed ice
   (extracted from pitted   Powdered ginger
   cherries or from red,
   canned cherries)

* If not available, add the powdered dry spice to the drink before shaking. Strain before serving.

Shake vigorously all ingredients except powdered ginger. Pour into 2 glasses. Sprinkle powdered ginger over each drink.

AUTUMN APPLE

The flavor of freshly extracted apple juice is especially delicate.

3 ounces apple juice
½ teaspoon grenadine
Sprinkling of powdered
clove

1 tablespoon crushed ice
Club soda
Slice of apple

Stir together juice, grenadine, clove, and ice until mixture is cold. Serve in 1 cocktail or juice glass. Fill to top with enough soda to make it fizz. Stir very lightly. Garnish with apple slice on rim of glass.

PRUNE APPLE (B)

Breakfast!

3 pitted prunes
¼ cup prune juice
1 cup apple juice

1 egg or ½ cup crushed
ice
Powdered cinnamon

Blend all ingredients on high speed for 20 seconds. Serve in 2 juice glasses.

APPLE SURPRISE (B)

A big treat for children's parties.

4 red apples   1 teaspoon honey
Juice of ½ orange   Dash lemon juice
½ cup frozen apple juice
  (defrosted, but still very
  cold) or cold, canned
  apple juice

Remove thick slice (for cover) from top of apples. Bore tiny
hole in same slices (for straw). Scoop out the inside of apples,
leaving the shells about ½ inch thick. Remove cores and pits.
Put shells into refrigerator. Blend apple pulp with other ingredients. Pour into chilled apple "cups." Cover with cut
slice. Insert short straw and serve immediately. Yields 1½
cups.

CRANBERRY LIME COOLER

¾ cup sugar   1 cup grapefruit juice
1½ cups water   1 cup ginger ale
3 cups cranberry juice   Ice cubes
  cocktail
Juice of 2 limes (save
  rind)

Boil sugar and water together for 5 minutes. Cool. Add to
juices. Stir. Add ginger ale. Pour over ice cubes in 6 glasses.
Garnish each with twist of rind.

PASTEL PINK (B)

I

1½ cups cranberry juice   1 egg white
1 tablespoon lemon juice   ½ cup cracked ice

Blend about 20 seconds and serve very cold in 2 glasses.

PASTEL PINK (B)

II

1½ cups cranberry juice   1 egg white
2 drops almond extract   ½ cup cracked ice

Blend about 20 seconds and serve very cold in 2 glasses.

CRANBERRY CREAM

Serve with small watercress sandwiches.

¾ cup cold cranberry juice
2 tablespoons sour cream
2 slices cucumber

Mix well or blend juice and cream. Serve cold in 2 juice glasses or nog cups. Garnish with cucumber slice.

PAPAYA CHERRY CREAM WHIP

½ cup chilled, canned papaya juice
½ cup chilled, canned cherry juice
1 rounded teaspoon whipped cream cheese

Beat or blend until juices and cheese are homogenized. Serve in 2 juice or cocktail glasses.

PAPAYA CHERRY MIX

½ cup chilled, canned papaya juice
½ cup chilled, canned cherry juice
Mace

Mix juices. Serve cold in 1 glass. Garnish with mace.

For other fruit juice drinks, see *Bogus Booze, Punch, (Other) Hot Shots*, and *Mostly Milk*.

JUICED FRUIT

MELON COCKTAIL (B)

1 slice sweet melon (as in 1 small portion)	3 tablespoons orange juice
	Dash grenadine
3 cut cherries (maraschino, canned, or fresh)	1 tablespoon chopped ice

Remove rind from melon. Put all but 1 small wedge of fruit cut from slice into container of electric blender. Add other ingredients. Blend until mixture is frothy. Pour into 1 cocktail glass and garnish rim with remaining sliver of melon. Serve with a short straw.

ROSE WHIRL (B)

Serve with fruit pancakes.

½ cup orange (cut up and peeled)

1 cup boysenberries or blackberries

⅛ cup white corn syrup

¼ peeled lemon

½ cup cracked ice

Blend until smooth. Strain through coarse strainer for seeds. Yields 3 juice glasses.

HAITIAN SPLASH (B)

1 mango (skinned and pitted)

⅓ banana

½ cup unsweetened grapefruit juice

½ teaspoon grenadine

Ice cubes

Blend ingredients together. Serve over ice cubes in 1 tall glass.

STRAWBERRY CRUSH (B)

½ cup sugared
   strawberries
   (canned, fresh, or
   frozen)

Juice of 1 lime
¼ cup water
¼ cup crushed ice
Thin slice of orange

Defrost strawberries if frozen. Blend strawberries, lime, water, and ice for about 10 seconds. Serve in 1 tall glass. Decorate with orange slice.

PINK RHUBARB (JE)

3 stalks rhubarb
½ cup strawberries

2 tablespoons crushed ice
2 teaspoons honey

Put rhubarb and strawberries through juice extractor. Pour over crushed ice in 1 tall glass. Add honey. Stir.

WHITE GRAPE COCKTAIL

A champagne substitute to be used with or without an occasion.

¼ pound white grapes
4 drops Angostura bitters

1 lump sugar
Club soda

Put grapes through juice extractor. Drop bitters on sugar and put into 1 champagne glass. Pour extracted grape juice over sugar. Add enough soda to give drink a slight fizz. Without disturbing the sugar, stir juice and soda slightly.

GIRL TALK (JE)

Serve with small, not-too-sweet cakes.

2 cups red grapes,   Honey to taste
  stemmed   Ice cubes
¼ lemon, peeled   Soda

Put grapes and lemon through juice extractor. Sweeten to taste with honey. Pour juice over ice in 2 glasses. Add soda. Stir lightly.

GRAPE COCKTAIL (JE)

1 cup seedless grapes   Honey to taste
1 small wedge fresh   Crushed ice
  pineapple

Put grapes and pineapple wedge through juice extractor. Stir in honey. Pour juice over crushed ice in 2 cocktail glasses. Garnish with green grapes on a pick.

PINK PEACH (B)

1 skinned peach (may be   1 tablespoon lime juice
  frozen, fresh, or canned) 1 tablespoon cracked ice
½ cup peach nectar   2 maraschino cherries
2 (or 3, to taste)
  tablespoons raspberry
  syrup

Blend all ingredients except cherries. Serve very cold in 2 old-fashioned glasses. Garnish each with a cherry.

NEAT PEACH (B)

½ cup frozen peaches   1 rounded teaspoon dried
  (defrosted but very   tarragon leaves
  cold) or 2 fresh peaches   Juice of 1 lemon
Juice of 2 oranges   2 rounded teaspoons honey

Put peaches through sieve. Shake all ingredients vigorously
and strain for leaves, or blend about 30 seconds until liquid
is rich and foamy. Serve in 4 small juice glasses.

VEGETABLE JUICE

NON-BLOODY MARY (D)

3 ounces tomato juice   Cracked ice
Juice of ½ lemon   Ice cube
Pinch salt   Sprig of mint
Pinch pepper
Pinch celery salt
½ teaspoon
  Worcestershire sauce

Shake all ingredients well with cracked ice. Strain into 1 old-
fashioned glass with ice cube. Garnish with mint.

Serve tomato drinks with salad of raw spinach tossed with
French dressing and crisp bacon bits.

VEGETABLE TOMATO (B) (D)

1 *small stalk celery*	1 *teaspoon* Worcestershire
1 *raw carrot*	*sauce*
3 *sprigs parsley*	½ *teaspoon salt*
2 *cups tomato juice*	*Crushed ice*
2 *tablespoons lemon juice*	3 *slices lemon*

Cut all vegetables into small pieces. Blend all ingredients except lemon slices on low speed for about 20 seconds, or until everything is liquefied. Pour over crushed ice in 3 glasses. Garnish with lemon slices.

Note: The vegetables may be put through the juice extractor. Add tomato juice, lemon juice, spices, and ice. Stir.

TOMATO JUICE COCKTAIL (B) (JE) OR (D)

1 *slice onion*	¼ *teaspoon orégano*
1 *thick slice green pepper*	*Dash Tabasco*
1 *teaspoon celery salt*	3 *cups tomato juice*
¼ *cup parsley clusters*	6 *slices lemon*

Blend all ingredients, except tomato juice and lemon, on low speed. Remove cover. Gradually add tomato juice. Chill. Serve in 6 juice glasses. Garnish each drink with slice of lemon.

Note: The vegetables may be put through a juice extractor. Then add the tomato juice and seasoning.

HERB CREAM TOMATO JUICE (B)

I

1 cup chilled tomato juice
1 teaspoon whipped cream cheese
¼ teaspoon dried basil

Blend all ingredients on high speed for 15 seconds. Serve cold in 1 glass.

HERB CREAM TOMATO JUICE (B)

II

1 cup chilled tomato juice
1 rounded tablespoon sour cream

⅛ teaspoon ginger powder
Fresh sprig of parsley

Blend juice, cream, and ginger for about 15 seconds. Garnish with parsley. Yields 1 glass.

HERB CREAM TOMATO JUICE

III

1½ cups canned tomatoes
½ cup heavy cream
Dash salt
Dash pepper

1 teaspoon dried basil leaves
Watercress
Ice cubes

Strain tomatoes through a sieve into a cocktail shaker. Add cream, salt, pepper, basil, and several ice cubes. Shake vigorously. Strain. Serve in juice glasses (4- to 6-ounce). Garnish with watercress. Serves 3.

3 sticks cinnamon, ½ kg white cloves

juice b. Sugar lemon. Tie

in small cheesecloth bag.

over heat ? 12 servings

Lemonade Punch

juice ⅔ C. Sugar

greenish
shaved
6 whole cloves broken
2 cinn sticks broken
1 lemon peel to 10 cups

...ulled Cider

...apple cider
...ed brown sugar
...nnamon, 1 tsp. whole cloves
...d ginger, 1 orange sliced
...ngredients & cover & heat
...for ? - Makes 10 to 12 serv.

...Apricot Punch
...icat Nectar
... 1/2 C brown sugar (packed)

BAVARIAN TOMATO COCKTAIL (D)

Follow with dinner of roast pork.

½ cup tomato juice
½ cup sauerkraut juice
⅛ teaspoon powdered caraway seed (or whole seed)

Mix all ingredients and serve in 2 juice glasses.

SAUERKRAUT COCKTAIL (D)

½ cup sauerkraut juice   Pinch salt
1½ cups tomato juice   Pinch coarsely ground
Dash lemon juice   black pepper
Dash Worcestershire sauce

Mix, chill, and serve in 4 cocktail glasses.

DUTCH DREAM (D)

An interesting beginning to a curry dinner.

1 cup canned carrot juice
1 cup sauerkraut juice
Dash curry powder

Mix all ingredients together. Serve very cold in 5 cocktail glasses.

B AND T IN A CUP (B)

1 cup tomato juice
2 slices broiled bacon
Black pepper

Blend juice and bacon for about ½ minute. Serve in 1 mug.
Sprinkle pepper on top.

TOMATO CLAM BLEND (B) (D)

A meal of sorts.

¾ cup tomato juice	¼ teaspoon horseradish
¾ cup clam juice	Crushed ice
3 fresh cherrystone clams	4 wedges lime

Blend together juices, clams, and horseradish for about 1
minute. Serve over crushed ice in 4 cocktail glasses. Stir.
Garnish with lime wedges.

PINK CLAM COCKTAIL (B) (D)

Follow with white steak fish.

¼ cup catsup	2 cups clam juice
1 thin slice onion	Ice cubes
1 stalk celery (coarsely cut)	4 slices lemon

Combine catsup, onion, celery, and about ½ cup clam juice.
Blend on high speed of electric blender for a few seconds.
Uncover and add remaining clam juice. Blend again briefly.
Pour over ice cubes in juice glasses (4- to 6-ounce). Garnish
with lemon slices. Serves 4.

ADULTS ONLY (B)

A sophisticated drink. Serve before a gourmet chicken or shellfish casserole.

4 ounces chilled clam
  juice
1 slice peeled avocado
1 teaspoon lime juice

¼ teaspoon dried thyme
  leaves
Pinch salt
Dash Tabasco

Blend all ingredients until thyme is almost pulverized. Serve cold in 1 large cocktail glass.

MARINA COCKTAIL (D)

½ cup chilled clam juice
¼ cup chilled, canned
  vegetable juice

¼ cup chilled sauerkraut
  juice
Dash Tabasco

Stir all ingredients together. Serve very cold in 1 juice glass.

GREEN GARDEN (JE) (D)

2 carrots
Handful of spinach
Handful of beet-greens
2 stalks celery, with tops
Several sprigs parsley

1 tomato
Sprig of fresh dill
Salt
Black pepper

Wash all vegetables well and cut into small pieces. (It is not necessary to scrape carrots.) Put through juice extractor. Add salt and pepper to taste. Yields 2 glasses.

GARDEN APPETIZER (JE) (D)

1 *medium cucumber* 4 *stalks celery*
1 *wedge medium onion* 1 *tablespoon lemon juice*
½ *green pepper* *Ice cubes*

Cut vegetables and put through juice extractor. Stir in lemon juice. Serve over ice cubes in 3 juice glasses.

PEP IN A GLASS (JE)

2 *medium mushrooms* ½ *pound fresh peas,*
2 *medium carrots* *shelled*
1 *bunch parsley stems*

Put all ingredients through juice extractor in order given. Serve cold in 2 cocktail glasses.

CUCUMBER CREAM (JE)

Serve with black or red caviar canapés.

1 *peeled cucumber* *Freshly ground black*
3 *sprigs fresh dill, with* *pepper, to taste*
stems 1 *teaspoon sour cream*
Pinch salt

Put cucumber and dill through juice extractor. Add salt and pepper. Top with dab of sour cream. Yields 1 glass.

BORSCHT BELT

Serve, before dinner, with small pumpernickel rounds with cream cheese and anchovy.

¾ cup cold borscht   *Slice of cucumber*
  (bottled will do)   *Chopped chives or dill*
2 tablespoons sour cream

Mix borscht and sour cream well, or blend, if beets are used. Garnish with cucumber slice that has been dipped into chives or dill. Serve in mug or nog cup.

FRUIT JUICE AND VEGETABLE JUICE MIXED

SANGRITA

1 cup tomato juice   *Tabasco to taste*
1 cup orange juice   *Cracked ice*

Mix juices, and add Tabasco. Serve over ice in 2 glasses.

PINEAPPLE PARSNIP (JE)

Parsnip juice (Who would believe it?) is sweet and smooth.

1 thick slice fresh pineapple
2 parsnips

Remove rind from pineapple. Cut pineapple and parsnips into small pieces and feed through juice extractor. Yields 1 glass.

PINEAPPLE PROTEIN PLUS (D)

One glass contains 150 calories.

1 cup fresh pineapple   *1 tablespoon brewers' yeast*
Handful of watercress
½ cup non-fat dry milk
   solids

Cut pineapple into small pieces. Put pineapple and watercress through juice extractor. Mix thoroughly with dry milk and brewers' yeast. Yields 2 glasses.

VEGETABLE FRUIT BLEND (B)

This is creamy, golden, and great.

1½ cups pineapple juice   *⅓ banana*
2 medium-size carrots,   *½ cup crushed ice*
   peeled and coarsely cut
   up

Blend all ingredients together in electric blender until thick and foamy. Pour into 8-ounce glasses. Serves 3.

FARM FROTH

Follow with a sautéed English Dover sole.

½ cup plus 2 tablespoons chilled, canned carrot juice
½ cup chilled apple juice
1 rounded tablespoon sour cream

Beat all ingredients thoroughly or blend on high speed for about 20 seconds. Serve in 2 juice glasses.

CAPRICOT (B)

½ cup dried apricots,
  sliced finely
  with scissors
1 diced, raw carrot

Juice of 1 lemon
2 cups water
Brown sugar to taste

Blend all ingredients. Serve very cold in 3 juice glasses.

Note: For richer flavor, use apricot nectar instead of water.

GRAPEFRUIT CARROT COCKTAIL (B)

3 carrots cooked in small
  amount of water, then
  cut up
¼ cup liquid in which
  carrots have been
  cooked

4 cups grapefruit juice
4 teaspoons grenadine
Dash powdered ginger
1½ cups shaved ice

Blend carrots with liquid a few seconds. Stop blender. Add other ingredients and blend until frothy. Serve immediately. Yields 6 glasses.

BEET TREAT

2 cups commercial borscht
(liquid only)
2 cups canned vegetable
juice

1 cup apple juice
⅛ teaspoon powdered
caraway seed
⅓ cucumber rind

Combine all ingredients except cucumber rind. Serve in 3 mugs. Garnish with cucumber rind.

Extracts, Essences, Etceteras

This chapter hovers nearest the lunatic fringe of non-drinking. There will be no hurt feelings if you do not rush to your nearest forest and pluck, then mash, as directed, eight ounces of small, wild violets for VIOLET AFSHOREH and rush back from the forest before your husband gets home from a board meeting at Univac, in order to serve it to him and to the Vice President of Sales whom he has brought home for dinner.

Although it is a lovely idea to serve flower-essence drinks at garden teas (the titillation of drinking one's own roses is not to be sniffed at), the recipes for which I have higher pragmatic hopes are the simple herb drinks, which are pleasantly odd, sophisticated, and, certainly, the least square, if you care, of the Zero Proofs.

HERB SOUR

⅓ cup water
2 teaspoons sugar (or to
   taste)
2 rounded teaspoons dried
   tarragon leaves
2 tablespoons lemon juice
2 tablespoons crushed ice

About ½ teaspoon egg
   white (or egg white
   substitute)
Club soda
Maraschino cherry
Slice of orange

Boil water in saucepan. Add sugar and tarragon leaves. Simmer several minutes on low flame. Let cool. Strain, pressing the tarragon leaves to get maximum liquid. Add lemon juice, ice, and egg white. Blend for about 20 seconds or shake vigorously in cocktail shaker. Pour into 1 sour glass and fill with soda. Stir once. Add cherry to drink and slice of orange on rim of glass.

SAFFRON COCKTAIL

⅓ cup water
1 teaspoon sugar (or to
   taste)
Pinch saffron

1½ tablespoons lemon
   juice
2 tablespoons chopped ice
Maraschino cherry

Boil water in saucepan. Add sugar and saffron. Simmer on very low flame several minutes, until yellow. Cool. Strain. Add juice and ice to liquid. Shake vigorously or blend briefly. Pour into 1 cocktail glass. Add cherry.

ROSEMARY

ater
ons sugar (or to

oons dried rosemary
espoons crushed ice

2 tablespoons lemon or
   lime juice
Twist of lemon or lime
   rind

ter in saucepan. Add sugar and rosemary. Simmer on
w flame for several minutes. Cool. Strain well. Add
d juice to liquid. Shake vigorously or blend for about
onds. Pour into 1 cocktail glass and add lemon or lime

JUMPING JUNIPER

2 rounded teaspoons dried
   juniper berries
⅓ cup water
2 teaspoons sugar (or to
   taste)

2 tablespoons chopped ice
2 tablespoons lime juice
Swirl of lime rind

Crush juniper berries in mortar. Add water. Or, put berries
and water in electric blender and blend until berries are broken
into tiny bits. Add sugar. Simmer over very low heat for
several minutes. Strain well. Cool. Add chopped ice and juice
to liquid. Shake vigorously or blend briefly. Pour into 1 cocktail glass. Garnish with lime rind.

PERSIAN MINT DRINK

½ cup sugar
½ cup white vinegar
Juice of ½ large lemon
2 tablespoons dried mint
    or
1 small bunch fresh mint
    or

4 drops mint extract
2 grated cucumbers
15 crushed almonds
Ice cubes
Cold water

Boil sugar and ¼ cup water until thick, but not syrupy. Add vinegar and lemon juice. When syrup barely drips from end of spoon, add mint leaves. Cook several minutes longer. Strain. (If mint extract is used instead of mint, add after liquid has cooled.) Add grated cucumbers and crushed almonds. Pour equal amounts of drink over ice cubes in 5 glasses. Fill with cold water.

JAIPUR GINGER

This is golden and bittersweet.

2 tablespoons ginger syrup (can be bought in oriental food
    shops, or see recipe*)
Ice cubes
Club soda

Pour ginger syrup over ice cubes in 1 tall glass. Fill glass with club soda. Stir.

*GINGER SYRUP

> 5 slices ginger
> 1 cup sugar
> 1 cup water

Boil all ingredients. Simmer about 45 minutes. Strain through wire sieve. If refrigerated, keep in tightly covered jar. Makes about 1 pint.

AFSHOREH

These are Persian and Syrian drinks made mostly of the extracts of aromatic flowers, seeds, and citrus peels. Serve them with meals (*not* the spaghetti or hamburger kind, naturally) or present them with biscuits as tea alternatives at summer meetings of the garden club.

ROSE DRINK

An overnight start is necessary before. I don't know what is necessary afterward. A strait jacket, perhaps.

> 3 tablespoons rose syrup*
> ½ glass crushed ice
> Club soda

Pour syrup over crushed ice in 1 tall glass. Add club soda. Stir gently.

*ROSE SYRUP

½ pound fresh rose leaves
1 pint boiling water
2 pounds sugar

Wash rose leaves carefully in cold water. Drain well. Add leaves to boiling water. Remove immediately from flame. (Do not cook.) Cover. Let stand about 10 hours. Strain through muslin jelly bag. Pour liquid into top of double boiler. Add sugar. Boil until syrup is clear. Cool. Keep in glass jar.

ROSE- OR ORANGE-BLOSSOM WATER AFSHOREH

2 tablespoons rose-flower   *1 tablespoon sugar*
water or 2 tablespoons   *Ice cubes*
orange-blossom water   *Cold water*

Combine all ingredients and serve in 1 large wineglass.

VIOLET AFSHOREH

2 cups water
8 ounces mashed, small, fresh, wild violets
2 cups sugar

Bring water to a boil. Add violets. Remove from heat immediately. Cover tightly. Let stand 12 hours. Strain liquid from violets into a measuring cup. Add equal amounts of sugar to flowers. Return liquid to violets and sugar. Pour into a double boiler. Cook over simmering water until sugar is dissolved. Serve in 4 very small cups or wineglasses.

SOUP

Why not?

SOUP AND SODA

1 can (10½ ounces)   Ice cubes
   condensed beef broth   Lemon peel
½ cup club soda

Combine beef broth and club soda. Pour over ice cubes in
3 tall glasses. Garnish with lemon peel.

SLOW SOUP FIZZ

This was somebody's idea at Campbell Soup. I had doubts,
but it works!

1 can (10½ ounces)   1 bottle (7 ounces) chilled
   condensed tomato soup   lemon-lime or club soda
½ soup can water   Cracked ice
1 tablespoon lemon juice   Lemon peel

Combine soup, water, and lemon juice. Stir to blend. Add soda
just before serving. Pour over cracked ice in 4 small glasses.
Garnish with twist of lemon peel.

BENGAL BROTH

Serve before a lamb dinner.

1 part bouillon
1 part tomato juice
Dash curry

Ice cubes
Slice of lemon

Mix together bouillon, juice, and curry. Pour over ice cubes in 1 small glass. Garnish with lemon.

*   *   *

TARZAN DINNER DRINK (B)

Good for children who won't eat, adults who can't, or just for laughs.

¼ pound lean, raw round
   steak
1 cup beef broth
   (may be canned
   bouillon)
2 thin slices onion

1 teaspoon lemon juice
1 strip green pepper, finely
   cut
½ stalk celery
Small branch of fresh
   parsley leaves

Scrape meat with a sharp knife. Blend everything except a bit of the parsley. Strain, or put through a food mill. Season to taste. Serve cold in 2 small mugs. Garnish with remaining parsley.

HORCHATA DE ALMENDRAS
(Spanish Almond Drink)

Serve with churros—crisp, fritterlike Spanish wafers.

60 almonds
1 quart water

4 ounces sugar
Crushed ice

Blanch almonds. Soak them for at least 12 hours. Strain and save water. Pound almonds in a mortar or blend them. Add almond water and sugar to taste. Serve in 6 cups with crushed ice.

COCONUT TROPICAL (B)

½ cup diced, peeled
  coconut
1 cup water

1 tablespoon sugar
1 cup cracked ice

Be sure that coconut is diced small enough for blender. Add water and sugar. Blend 20 seconds. Strain, and while doing so press coconut with back of spoon to extract all the milk. Return liquid to blender. Add ice. Cover. Blend again to smooth, rich consistency. Serve in cocktail glasses or coconut shells with short straws. Yields about 4 glasses.

Bogus Booze

Some bogus boozes are extracts and might well be in the preceding chapter, but it seems to me all drinks whose primary purpose is fakery should be kept together—like crooks.

Bogus booze can lose in the imitation process. Anything geared at being like something else, instead of being just *good*, usually sacrifices some of its goodness for some of its likeness. There are, I am sure, better things unfermented grapes can do besides trying to seem like fermented grapes. And rum extract, while it does approximate a rum attitude, does not taste great. But neither does rum, *I* don't think.

Having knocked the product, I now feel free to say that some of the non-spirits are really not bad. Besides, achieving a likeness sometimes outweighs other considerations: At a wedding reception, the champagne connotation (not so much the champagne itself) can make champagne worth imitating.*

* See BRIDE'S BOWL.

Bogus booze works, too, as an attractive bridge between the arts of drinking and non-drinking. This chapter names some of the best and/or best-known of the bogus booze bunch. Recipes are here and there if you should get the urge to do more than pour. (With extracts, of course, you *have* to do more than pour.) Whenever possible, the masquerade should be enhanced.

The following fakes should be treated with the utmost of alcoholic courtesies and appurtenances—silver wine coolers, crystal—the more flourishes, the better.

Note: When used appropriately (a few drops), the alcohol content of extracts and of the various bitters and flavoring agents does not result in an alcoholic drink. An alcoholic drink, as mentioned earlier, contains more than one-half of 1% alcohol.

Since there are about 60 drops to a teaspoon, 6 teaspoons to an ounce, 18 teaspoons in a 3-ounce cocktail glass, and 1080 drops in a cocktail glass, 6 drops of an extract, high alcohol content notwithstanding, counts for nil.

PSEUDO WINES, SPARKLING AND STILL

Most non-alcoholic wines are about $2.50 for a 10-ounce bottle. They can be bought at gourmet shops and are usually packaged (perhaps I should say costumed) beautifully.

MEIER'S CATAWBA GRAPE JUICE
Domestic. Still or sparkling. Has more oomph than most.

LE CHÂTEAU DU RHIN

RIMUSS GRAPE JUICE

PERLANDER TRAUBENSAFT
A pure white grape juice from West Germany.

TIARA CELEBRATION CHAMPAGNE GRAPE JUICE
Domestic, and a more than reasonable facsimile.

MOCK WINE CUP

Ice cubes
½ orange, sliced
¼ lemon, sliced
2 slices pineapple

1 ounce liquid from
  maraschino cherries
1 ten-ounce bottle
  non-alcoholic white wine

Half fill glass pitcher with ice cubes. Add fruit, maraschino juice, and wine. Serve in champagne glasses. Yields about 5 glasses.

CUCUMBER WINE PUNCH

3 cups non-alcoholic,
  still white wine
1 can frozen lemonade
  concentrate

6 strips cucumber rind
1 quart tea*
Ice cubes

Mix wine, lemonade concentrate, and cucumber rind with tea. Remove rind after 5 minutes. Serve in punch bowl over ice cubes. Yields about 15 punch cups.

* See Hot Tea recipe.

NON-ROSE COCKTAIL

Dash Rose's* lime juice　　*Maraschino cherry*
Ice cubes　　　　　　　　*Slice of orange*
Still, non-alcoholic rosé
　wine

Add dash lime juice to ice cubes in 1 very tall glass. Fill
with wine. Garnish with cherry and orange slice.

NEGUS

Bogus booze works well in hot drinks, when you can't tell
what it is.

1 bottle non-alcoholic wine　*12 slices lemon*
½ pint club soda　　　　　*Nutmeg*
2 quarts boiling water

Mix together all ingredients except nutmeg. Serve in 12 mugs.
Grate nutmeg on top of each.

MOCK BISHOP

This is hot, too.

1 orange
About 20 cloves
4 cups non-alcoholic wine

* A special kind of lime juice.

Stick orange with cloves. Place in pan and heat thoroughly in oven. Cut orange into quarters, and put into top section of double boiler (preferably glass). Pour wine over orange. Simmer on very low heat for 15 minutes. Serve hot in 4 small mugs.

MOCK CHAMPAGNE COCKTAIL

1 *small lump sugar*
4 *dashes Angostura bitters*
Dash lemon juice

Non-alcoholic champagne, chilled
Spiral rind of ½ lemon

Place sugar in 1 champagne glass. Saturate with bitters. Add lemon juice and champagne. Do not stir. Garnish with lemon spiral.

BRIDE'S BOWL

Juice of 2 lemons
1 *cubed pineapple, dredge with 1 cup sugar*
4 *cups canned, or cubed pineapple (do not add sugar)*
Ice block
1 *quart sparkling water*

1 *quart lightly sugared fresh strawberries*
or
1 *quart frozen whole strawberries, thawed (without syrup)*
2 *fifths non-alcoholic champagne*

Add lemon juice to pineapple. Let stand about 20 minutes. Pour into punch bowl, over ice block. Add sparkling water. Just before serving, add strawberries and champagne. Yields about 25 punch cups.

Some winelike apple juices:

GOLDEN PIPPIN SPARKLING APPLE JUICE
An English pseudo-champagne made of fresh apples. (See
APPLE SURPRISE in the fruit juice section.) The drink
can be made for adults by substituting sparkling apple juice
for the other kind.

LEHR'S APPLE JUICE
The GRAPE (red or white) and RED CURRANT are good too.
Pour into a frosted glass over crushed ice.

CIDRO-MOUSSEUX SPARKLING APPLE JUICE
Canadian.

APPELLA GOLDEN APPLE JUICE
Danish.

TAUNTON'S STILL CIDER
English.

RED APPLE COCKTAIL

*⅔ cup sparkling apple
juice
⅓ cup non-alcoholic
sparkling red wine*

*Cracked ice
Dash Angostura bitters
Wedge of apple
Powdered cinnamon*

Pour juice and wine over ice in 2 cocktail glasses. Add bitters.
Stir. Garnish with wedge of apple, dipped in cinnamon.

"LIQUEURS" OR "CORDIALS"

SPICE ISLAND CORDIALS MANY FLAVORS

GET MINT
French crème de menthe substitute.

ORLIN'S CHERRI BERRI AND KRÈME DE MENTHE
From Montreal. Cherry Heering and crème de menthe facsimiles.

These are sweet, syrupy, not *heartily* recommended unless you like things sweet and syrupy. If so, serve them in cordial glasses over shaved ice. They may also be added to fruit juice (lemon or lime works best), or to club soda.

CHERRI JULEP

Non-alcoholic cherry   *Club soda*
   cordial   *Sprig of mint*
Ice cubes

Pour 1 wineglass of cordial over ice cubes in 1 tall glass. Fill with club soda. Add mint.

ALMOST ALEXANDER

2 tablespoons non-alcoholic crème de cacao
Strong, cold coffee
Cream

Pour crème de cacao into wineglass. Fill almost to top with coffee. Mix. Float cream on top. (For less sweet drink use less crème de cacao.)

NON-ALCOHOLIC CREME DE MENTHE FRAPPE

Shaved ice
Non-alcoholic crème de menthe

Fill 1 wine or cocktail glass with ice. Pour crème de menthe over ice.

CHERRY RICKEY

2 jiggers non-alcoholic   *Cracked ice*
*   cherry cordial*   *Club soda*
1½ jiggers lemon or lime
*   juice*

Mix cherry cordial, juice, and ice in 1 tall glass. Add club soda. Stir.

RULLES SWEDISH ARRAK PUNSCH
Sweet, pungent, rum-flavored. Good for nogs and punches.

SPICE ISLAND ARRACK
Similar to above, not quite as good.

TAHITIAN TINGLE

¼ cup orange juice   *Crushed ice*
¼ cup pineapple juice   *Spear of fresh or canned*
¼ cup peach nectar   *   pineapple*
1 tablespoon lemon juice
1 tablespoon non-alcoholic
*   arrack*

Stir together juices and arrack. Serve in 1 tall glass over crushed ice. Garnish with pineapple spear.

SCOTCH IRISH COFFEE

1 cup strong, hot coffee (instant coffee may be used)
2 tablespoons non-alcoholic arrack
1½ tablespoons sweet cream

Mix coffee and arrack in 1 Irish coffee glass or mug. Float cream on top. Serve immediately.

COFFEE GROG (B)

2 tablespoons butter
¾ cup brown sugar
Dash salt
⅛ teaspoon powdered cinnamon
⅛ teaspoon powdered nutmeg
⅛ teaspoon powdered allspice
⅛ teaspoon powdered cloves
1 teaspoon non-alcoholic arrack
2 tablespoons sweet cream
1 strip lemon rind
1 strip orange rind
¾ cup hot coffee

Cream together butter and sugar. Add salt. Blend. Add spices. Blend again thoroughly. Measure 1 tablespoon of mixture (grog base)* into 2 mugs. Add arrack, cream, and rinds. Stir in hot coffee.

* May be stored in refrigerator.

GINGER BEER

Schweppes bottles this English product. Should be drunk cold.

THE EXTRACTS

Burnett's, McCormick, and Ehlers are the best-known. Of these, the most successful flavors are (however mild) rum, brandy, and whiskey.

CAFE BRULOT

6 *pieces lump sugar*
6 *whole cloves*
1 *one-inch stick cinnamon*
1 *large lemon peel*
1 *demitasse cup freshly boiled water*
4 *cups hot demitasse coffee*
5 *drops brandy extract*

Stir sugar, cloves, cinnamon, lemon peel, and water in chafing dish for about 5 minutes. Add coffee and extract. Serve immediately in 6 demitasse cups.

MOCK WHISKEY EGGNOG

Good Christmas drink for children.

6 *eggs*
4 *tablespoons sugar*
6 *cups milk*
3 *teaspoons vanilla*
1½ *teaspoons whiskey extract*
Dash *nutmeg*

Beat eggs and sugar. Add milk, vanilla, and whiskey flavor. Beat again. Top with nutmeg. Serve cold in 12 punch cups.

PHONY ISLAND RUM

½ mashed banana
½ cup cold pineapple
   juice
1 teaspoon grenadine
4 drops rum extract

Part of egg white, or
   several drops
   egg white substitute
Shaved ice
Maraschino cherry

Shake all ingredients, except cherry, vigorously in cocktail shaker. Serve in 1 tall glass and garnish with cherry.

Punch

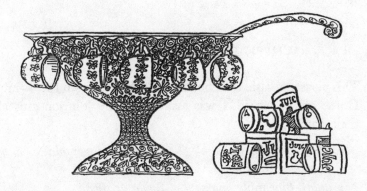

Wonders are ceaseless. I was on a Fifth Avenue bus, eyes front, headed for the library at Forty-second Street (I am there now) where it was my intention to delve into punch via the written word. I looked up, past two clothed elbows, at the ads, expecting to read about how nice it is to be a blonde, when there, instead, was a comprehensive treatise on punch, accompanied by a line drawing of two old gentlemen in embroidered britches looking at a big cut-glass bowl. In articulate Miss-Subways prose, I was informed that punch originated in India; that the word "punch" came from "pauch," meaning five; that punch was composed, originally, of five ingredients—and that the wassail bowl is "terribly merry." All of which has made me think twice about my previously poor attitude regarding public transportation in New York City. How can one complain when, for all one knows, as one sits here in the archives verifying the bus data, the epistemology of egg creams is being glued up in the first three cars of the downtown IRT?

Note: The bus information was correct. Of course, punch is no longer limited to five ingredients. As far as I can tell, the best definition of punch goes like the Who's-buried-in-Grant's-tomb joke: What's in a punch bowl is punch, and vice versa.

WHITE HOUSE ORANGE PUNCH

This pleasant, basic fruit punch came directly from the White House and is served, I was assured, by the Johnson girls at their parties.

1 gallon orange juice	2 quarts ginger ale
1 quart lemon juice	Ice block
1 quart pineapple juice	Sugar to taste
1 gallon water	

Pour juices, water, and ginger ale over block of ice in large punch bowl. Sweeten to taste and stir. Serves 50.

MICHIGAN GUBERNATORIAL PUNCH

This came from Mrs. George W. Romney.

Water or ginger ale	1 can frozen pineapple
1 can frozen lime juice	juice concentrate
concentrate	Pint lime sherbet
1 can frozen lemon juice	
concentrate	

Add water to fruit juice concentrates, slightly less than as directed on can, or for a fizzier, sweeter punch, substitute ginger ale. Pour over block of ice in punch bowl. Add sherbet last. Yields about 40 punch cups.

PROM PUNCH

1 ten-ounce package frozen strawberries
1 eight-ounce can crushed pineapple
1 six-ounce can frozen lemonade concentrate
3 quarts cold ginger ale
1 tray crushed ice

Partially defrost strawberries. Combine in punch bowl with pineapple and lemonade concentrate. Stir until lemonade is liquefied. Add ginger ale and ice. Serve immediately. Yields about 20 punch cups.

FRUIT FIZZ PUNCH

5 cups ginger ale
5 cups tonic
1 cup unsweetened pineapple juice
1 cup pineapple chunks (fresh, canned, or frozen)
1 cup sugared strawberries
Juice of ½ lemon
1 tray ice cubes

All liquids should be very cold. Pour all ingredients over ice cubes in a punch bowl. Yields 20 punch cups liquid before ice is added.

PINK HONEY PUNCH

2½ cups orange juice
2 cups unsweetened
    pineapple juice
½ cup lemon juice
½ cup maraschino cherry
    juice

¼ cup honey
Ice block
2 cups cold ginger ale

Combine juices and honey. Refrigerate. When ready to serve, pour over ice block in punch bowl. Add ginger ale. Stir. Yields 10 to 12 punch cups.

PARTY PUNCH

I

1 pint pineapple juice
1 pint grape juice
12 cups black raspberry
    soda

Ice cubes
Sprigs of mint

Combine juices, soda, and ice cubes. Garnish with mint. Yields about 20 punch cups.

PARTY PUNCH

II

This one is less sweet.

1 pint pineapple juice
1 pint loganberry juice
12 cups black cherry soda
1 pint strong, very cold tea

Ice cubes
Sprigs of mint

Combine juices, soda, tea, and ice cubes. Garnish with mint. Yields about 20 punch cups.

SPARKLING FRUIT PUNCH

1 orange, sliced
¼ banana, sliced thin
1 bottle maraschino cherries
1 cup tiny seedless white grapes (may be canned)
1 dozen fresh strawberries, sliced thin, or
1 twelve-ounce package frozen strawberries

2 trays ice cubes
2 large bottles orange soda
2 large bottles lemon soda

Quarter each slice of orange. Place all fruit and ice cubes in punch bowl. Pour beverages over all and stir briefly. Serve promptly. Yields about 25 punch cups.

TERRACE PUNCH

1 *pineapple*   6 *cups orange juice*
2 *cups raspberry syrup*   Ice block
2 *cups lime juice*   3 *quarts club soda*

Peel pineapple. Remove core and cut into bite-size pieces. Let stand several hours in punch bowl with all other ingredients except ice and club soda. When ready to serve, add ice block, then club soda. Yields about 35 punch cups.

FRUIT SHERBET PUNCH

1 *pint grape juice*   4 *cups club soda*
⅓ *cup lemon juice*   1 *pint lemon or banana*
⅓ *cup orange juice*   *sherbet*
½ *cup sugar*

Combine juices and sugar. Stir until sugar is dissolved. Chill. When ready to serve, add club soda. Float scoops of sherbet on top. Yields about 8 cups.

MEXICAN FRUIT PUNCH

This has to be prepared 3 days ahead of time. Serve at a taco party.

1 *pineapple*   4 *quarts water*
½ *cup tamarind, peeled*   2 *cups sugar*
  (*can be bought at*   2 *sticks cinnamon*
  Spanish grocery)   8 *whole cloves*
2½ *cups orange juice*

Wash pineapple well. Remove rind and save. Grate pineapple meat. Coarsely chop ½ of the rind. Combine all ingredients. Refrigerate in a tightly covered jar for about 3 days. Strain well. Serve very cold. Yields about 25 to 30 punch cups.

FINNISH PUNCH BOWL

Has to be started a day early.

2 cups cherry or raspberry
juice
2 lemons, sliced thin
1 orange, peeled and
sliced

1 pineapple
½ cup blanched almonds
5 tablespoons sugar
4 cups club soda
1 tray ice cubes

Pour cherry or raspberry juice into punch bowl. Add lemons and orange. Peel pineapple, cut meat into small cubes, and add to punch bowl. Add almonds split in half, and enough sugar to make the mixture rather sweet. Cover bowl and refrigerate overnight. Just before serving, add club soda and ice. Yields about 20 punch cups.

GRADUATION PUNCH (B)

¼ cup drained
maraschino
cherries
1½ cups pitted apricots
with juice (28-ounce
can)

¼ cup lemon juice
1 gallon chilled
unsweetened pineapple
juice
Ice block

Blend cherries, apricots, 1 cup apricot juice (from can), and lemon juice for 2 minutes, or until liquefied. Add pineapple juice and remaining apricot juice. Stir. Serve over ice block in punch bowl. Yields about 40 punch cups.

RHUBARB PUNCH

3 *pounds rhubarb*
2 *quarts water*
2½ *cups sugar*
1½ *cups orange juice*
¾ *cup shredded pineapple*
2 *trays ice cubes*

Wash rhubarb and cut into small pieces. Simmer in water until soft. Strain. Measure water from cooked rhubarb, and add enough cold water to make 2 quarts. Add sugar and stir until dissolved. Add orange juice and pineapple. Chill. Add ice cubes before serving. Yields about 30 punch cups.

MELON PUNCH BOWL

I think the melon-bowl idea is corny, but it helps if you don't have a punch bowl.

½ *watermelon*
Water
3 *six-ounce cans frozen lemonade concentrate*
½ *cantaloupe*
¼ *honeydew melon*

Scoop out pink, edible part of watermelon with a sharp knife. Serrate edge of melon. Add water to lemonade concentrate, as directed on can, and pour into watermelon shell. Float small scoops of the 3 melons on top. Yields about 14 punch cups.

WATERMELON FROTH PUNCH (B)

Strictly summer.

Chunks of seeded watermelon	1 cup orange juice
	Crushed ice
Juice of 1 lime	8 sprigs mint

Fill blender container with most of watermelon chunks. Cover and turn on high speed. Remove cover, and with motor on, drop in more watermelon until liquid almost fills container. Pour into small punch bowl. Add lime juice and orange juice. Stir. Serve immediately over crushed ice in 8 punch cups. Garnish with mint sprigs.

BLUE PUNCH (B)

For a blue debut.

5 cups blueberries	11 cups water
Rind of ½ orange	1 tablespoon cornstarch
Rind of 1 lime	Whipped cream (optional)
1-inch stick of cinnamon	Powdered cinnamon
½ cup sugar	

Simmer berries, rinds, cinnamon stick, and sugar in 10 cups of water until berries are soft. Strain. Save liquid. Blend berries. Combine blended berries with liquid. Mix cornstarch in

1 cup of water. Add to liquid. Simmer 6 minutes, then chill. Pour in punch bowl. Garnish with whipped cream and/or powdered cinnamon. Yields about 15 punch cups.

HOLIDAY CURRANT PUNCH

I

1 cup red currant jelly
1 cup boiling water
½ cup grenadine
1 six-ounce can frozen
   limeade concentrate

1 six-ounce can frozen
   grapefruit juice
   concentrate

Beat jelly with a fork until it is well broken up, then beat with a rotary beater. Add boiling water. Continue to beat, until jelly is dissolved. Add grenadine. Add water to juice concentrates as directed on cans. Add jelly-grenadine mixture. Chill in refrigerator. Serve over ice block in punch bowl. Yields about 12 punch cups.

HOLIDAY CURRANT PUNCH

II

2 cups currant jelly
2 cups boiling water
2 cups pineapple juice
½ cup lemon juice

½ cup orange juice
2 cups lime juice
Ice mold
1 quart ginger ale

Beat jelly until frothy. Add boiling water. Beat again until jelly has dissolved. Add all fruit juices. Chill in refrigerator. Pour over ice mold in punch bowl. Add ginger ale. Stir. Serve immediately. Yields about 20 punch cups.

ICE CREAM PUNCH

1 quart ice cream (vanilla or any fruit flavor)
1½ cups lemon juice
1 cup pineapple juice

1½ cups sugar
2 trays ice cubes
2 large bottles chilled club soda

Scoop ice cream into balls. Place on tray and keep in freezer until ready to use. Stir juices and sugar until sugar has dissolved. Chill. When ready to serve, pour juice mixture over ice cubes in punch bowl. Add club soda. Stir briefly. Add ice cream balls. Yields about 20 punch cups.

CHURCH PUNCH FOR 100

Pretty uncontroversial, as it stands. Innovations are invited.

10 cups boiling water
1 cup loose tea or 32 tea bags
6 pints lemon juice
5 quarts orange juice
5¼ pounds sugar

4½ gallons sparkling water
Ice cubes or ice block
100 green minted cherries (optional)
20 lemons, sliced thin

Pour boiling water over tea and steep 6 minutes. Strain. Pour into large bowl. Add lemon juice, orange juice, and sugar.

Stir until sugar dissolves. When ready to serve, pour sparkling water over ice cubes or ice block. Garnish with cherries and lemon slices on picks.

Note: Other punches in *Bogus Booze* and *Tea.*

DRINKS FOR
AFTER DINNER AND
LONG BEFORE

Coffee

Until about the eighteenth century, coffee could still be found at the apothecary, where it was shelved with the other dropsy cures. Early in the eleventh century a Muhammadan doctor published the news that coffee "fortifies the members, cleanses the skin, dries up the humidities that are under it, and gives an excellent smell to all the body."

While it is still employed by many people as a morning transfusion, coffee has long since been edged out of medicinal circles.

Coffee, now, is the period at the end of the lunch or dinner sentence; or, as an Arcadian friend put it, "Coffee is what you do when you sit around, when you're not sitting around Drinking."

Since the point of drinking coffee usually has little to do with the enjoyment of the beverage itself, the result is: There's coffee—and there's *coffee*. This chapter is about the second kind.

The first kind you don't have to read books for.

HOT

The Rules in General

1. Begin with a thoroughly clean coffee maker.
2. Use fresh coffee. (Buy the size can or package that will be used up within a week after opening.)
3. Use fresh water.
4. Try to use the full or near-full capacity of the coffee maker.
5. Serve immediately after making.
6. If reheating is necessary, be careful not to boil the coffee.

The general rule for American coffee is 2 level measuring tablespoonfuls of coffee to each ¾ cup (6 fluid ounces) of water for each serving. Slightly more or less coffee should be used, depending on the strength desired.

THREE COFFEE-MAKING METHODS

PERCOLATOR

Measure fresh cold water into percolator. Place on heat until water boils. Remove from heat. Measure regular-grind coffee into basket. Insert basket into percolator, cover, return to heat, percolate slowly 6 to 8 minutes. Remove coffee basket and serve.

DRIP

Pre-heat pot by rinsing with very hot water. Measure drip-grind coffee into filter section. Measure fresh boiling water into upper container. Cover. When dripping is completed, re-move upper section. Stir brew and serve. To keep coffee very hot, keep pot over very small flame. DO NOT BOIL.

VACUUM

Measure fresh cold water into lower bowl of coffee maker. Place on heat. Place filter in upper bowl. Add vacuum-grind coffee. When water boils, reduce flame or turn off electricity. Insert upper bowl with slight twist. Let most of water rise into upper bowl. Stir water and coffee thoroughly. In 1 to 3 minutes, remove from heat. When brew returns to lower bowl, remove upper bowl and serve.

COFFEE FOR FIFTY

1 pound regular-grind coffee
2 gallons water

Into a cheesecloth or muslin bag, large enough to hold at least twice the amount, put coffee. Bring water to a boil in a large pot. Immerse coffee in pot. Cover tightly. Reduce heat. Do not boil. Simmer 15 minutes. Dip bag up and down several times, then remove bag. Cover to keep coffee hot.

ESPRESSO COFFEE

Espresso coffee, which is very fine and dark, should be made in an espresso machine under steam pressure, but a *macchinetta*, the Italian drip pot, will do.

1½ cups boiling water   4 twists lemon rind
8 level tablespoons French   Lump sugar (optional)
   or Italian roast drip-grind
   coffee

Pour boiling water into lower cylinder of *macchinetta*. Measure coffee into sieve. Put together, placing spout cylinder on top. Place on heat. When steam emerges from small opening in lower cylinder, remove from heat and turn *macchinetta* upside down. When all the brew has dripped through, the coffee is ready. Serve in 4 demitasse cups. Add lemon twists to each, and lump sugar, if desired.

COFFEE CAPPUCCINO

½ cup hot espresso coffee   Cinnamon
½ cup steaming milk   Nutmeg
Sugar

Mix coffee and milk in 1 cup. Add sugar to taste. Sprinkle cinnamon and nutmeg on top.

CAFE AU LAIT

Serve in the morning, with croissants.

½ cup strong, hot coffee
½ cup hot milk

Use 2 pots, or coffeepot and pitcher. Pour simultaneously into 1 cup.

VIENNESE COFFEE

Serve with Sacher Torte.

1 cup strong, hot coffee
Sugar to taste
1 rounded teaspoon rich whipped cream

Serve coffee, sweetened to taste, in 1 regular coffee cup. Top with whipped cream.

HOT MOCHA JAVA

½ cup hot coffee
½ cup hot cocoa
1 marshmallow

Combine coffee and cocoa. Serve in 1 mug. Top with marshmallow.

COFFEE KAHULUI

1⅓ cups flaked coconut   1¼ cups boiling water
1⅓ cups milk   2 drops vanilla extract
2 tablespoons instant   1 teaspoon sugar
     coffee powder

Simmer coconut and milk for about 3 minutes until foamy. Separate coconut from milk by straining. Put coconut on cookie sheet, and bake for 10 minutes at 350° F. (moderate). Shake pan occasionally. Meanwhile, dissolve coffee in boiling water. Add coconut-flavored milk, vanilla, and sugar. Stir. Serve in small mugs and sprinkle each with toasted coconut. Serves 4.

COFFEE CHOCOLACCINO

2 cups hot espresso coffee   Whipped cream
2 teaspoons chocolate   Shaved sweet chocolate
     syrup

Combine coffee and syrup in 2 cups. Top with whipped cream and shaved chocolate.

HOT MOCHA FROTH (B)

1 cup hot coffee
½ cup heavy cream
¼ cup semisweet chocolate bits

Combine coffee and cream and beat over low heat until steaming hot. Pour into blender; add chocolate bits. Cover tightly and blend on high speed for 20 seconds. Pour into warm mugs. Serves 2.

TURKISH COFFEE

Serve with platter of sesame candies and Turkish paste.

1½ cups water
4 tablespoons Turkish coffee (finely pulverized)
4 teaspoons sugar

Measure water into a heavy saucepan. Add coffee and sugar. Bring to a boil. Allow brew to "froth up" 3 times. Remove from heat. Add a few drops of cold water. Serve in 2 very small cups. Top each drink with coffee foam.

COFFEE ALMONDINE

4 drops almond extract
Sugar to taste
1 cup hot coffee
2 tablespoons whipped cream

1 teaspoon dried mixed fruit (fruitcake variety)

Add extract and sugar to coffee in 1 cup. Stir. Top coffee with whipped cream, sprinkle dried fruit on cream.

MID-EASTERN COFFEE

Serve with oriental honey cakes.

12 cardamon seeds
4 cups hot, strong coffee
Sugar to taste

Crack cardamon seeds. Place 3 in the bottom of each of 4 cups. Add coffee and sweeten to taste.

COFFEE CREOLE

This is *very* strong.

12 tablespoons dark-roast coffee, with chicory added
4 cups boiling water

Make coffee according to drip method, but pour water in very gradually, about 2 tablespoons at a time. Makes 3½ or 3 generous cups.

PINK AND WHITE DESSERT COFFEE

1 cup hot coffee
1 tablespoon whipped cream
1½ teaspoons raspberry syrup

Pour hot coffee into 1 heavy stemmed glass (with small coffee spoon in it). Float cream on top. Pour syrup very slowly over cream. Do not stir.

COLD

ICED COFFEE

Brew coffee, double-strength. Pour it in tall glasses filled with ice cubes. Serve with cream and extra-fine sugar, or with sugar syrup.

ICE CUBE COFFEE

Make regular coffee. Pour into ice cube trays. Freeze. Pour freshly brewed coffee over coffee ice cubes in tall glasses. Serve with cream and sugar.

INSTANT ICED COFFEE FOR ONE

Mix 2 teaspoons instant coffee in ½ cup of cold water. Pour into 1 tall glass. Stir. Add ice cubes, cream, and extra-fine sugar.

INSTANT ICED COFFEE FOR FIFTY

1 *gallon boiling water*	*Ice cubes (regular or*
1 *six-ounce jar instant*	*coffee)*
coffee	*Pitcher of cream*
1 *gallon cold water*	*Bowl of sugar*

Pour boiling water over coffee. Mix well. Add cold water. Stir thoroughly. Pour over ice cubes in tall glasses. Serve cream and sugar separately.

ICED ESPRESSO

Hot espresso coffee   *Simple sugar syrup*
Cracked ice   *Curl of lemon peel*

Pour hot espresso into 1 small stemmed glass filled with
cracked ice. Sweeten to taste with syrup. Garnish with lemon
peel curl.

COFFEE FROTH (B) (D)

2 cups cracked ice
1 cup extra-strong, cool coffee
1 tablespoon granulated sugar (or sugar substitute)

Half fill electric blender container with finely chopped ice.
Add coffee and sugar. (For a non-caloric drink, use sugar substitute.) Blend until thick and foamy. Serve in 4 tall glasses.

DIETETIC MOCHA FROTH (B) (D)

COFFEE FROTH plus 2 tablespoons low-calorie chocolate
syrup.

MOCHA FROST

2½ cups strong, cold coffee
5 tablespoons chocolate syrup
1 pint soft coffee ice cream

Beat or blend all ingredients. When smooth and creamy, serve in 4 tall glasses.

BITTERS AND ICED COFFEE

This is coffee's answer to hard liquor.

2½ cups iced coffee   *Angostura bitters*
   (see ICED COFFEE)   *Club soda*
Ice cubes

Pour coffee over ice cubes in 4 tall glasses. Add 4 drops bitters to each. Fill glasses with club soda. Stir.

APRICOT CREAM COFFEE

1⅓ cups chilled coffee   *⅔ cup milk*
1 cup softened coffee ice   *¼ teaspoon almond*
  cream   *extract*
1 cup chilled apricot
  nectar

Combine all ingredients and beat thoroughly with a rotary beater or blend in an electric blender. Serve with straws in small glasses (4- to 6-ounce). Serves 4.

THE PENNSYLVANIA MOCHA

¼ cup instant coffee
1½ tablespoons cocoa
¼ cup sugar
2 cups water
2 cups (3 small cans)
    evaporated milk

⅛ teaspoon vanilla
Ice cubes
Grated chocolate

Simmer coffee, cocoa, sugar, and water several minutes. Stir constantly. Add evaporated milk and vanilla. Stir. Chill. Serve over ice cubes in 6 five-ounce glasses. Sprinkle top of each with shaved chocolate.

MAPLE COFFEE ICE

½ cup maple syrup
4 cups strong coffee
Coffee ice cubes (see
    ICE CUBE COFFEE)

1 cup whipped cream
Grated orange peel

Stir syrup in coffee. Pour over ice cubes in 5 glasses. Top each with whipped cream and a dash of orange peel.

FROSTED COFFEE HAWAII

2 cups strong, cold coffee
1 cup chilled pineapple juice
1 pint soft vanilla ice cream

Beat or blend all ingredients. When smooth and foamy, pour into 4 tall glasses.

COFFEE NECTAR

2½ cups strong, cold coffee
1 pint coffee ice cream
1 tablespoon Angostura bitters

Beat or blend all ingredients. When smooth and foamy, pour into 4 tall glasses.

COLA COFFEE

2 tablespoons cream   *1 cup pre-cooled coffee*
Ice cubes   *¼ cup cola*

Pour cream over ice cubes in 1 glass. Add coffee. Fill glass with cola. Stir briefly.

ICE AND SPICE COFFEE

The recipe must be started an hour before serving. This is a sophisticated, not very sweet drink, good for morning meetings.

2 cinnamon sticks   *Ice cubes*
  (broken up)   *Sugar to taste*
6 cloves   *Cream*
6 allspice berries
3 cups hot, double-
  strength coffee

Tie spices securely into cheesecloth bag. Drop bag into hot coffee. Let stand approximately one hour. Remove bag. Pour over ice in 4 tall glasses. Add sugar and cream to taste.

CARDAMON COFFEE

6 thin slices banana   1½ tablespoons cream
1 cup strong, iced coffee   Powdered cardamon
Sugar to taste

Mash banana. Add coffee, sugar, and cream. Beat until frothy or blend all ingredients. Serve in 1 tall glass and sprinkle cardamon on top.

Tea

It's my book and I can say something ridiculous if I want to and I want to: TEA IS FEMALE COFFEE. I know that that is a belief irrationally held (tattooed men drink tea constantly, I am sure), but not even a psychiatrist can convince me otherwise. You see, I *like* believing that tea is female coffee. I find it infinitely groovier than thinking tea is the dried leaf of an evergreen plant which, at its best, grows slowly in high altitudes of about five thousand feet, thereby producing, according to the district where it grows, over fifteen hundred teas, of which there are three types, black, green, and oolong, which, in turn, are blended and processed until, when we buy black tea, for instance, we are really buying a blend of twenty or thirty black teas.

Who cares?

BETTER-KNOWN TEAS

Black (comprises 97% of the tea consumed in the U.S.)

ASSAM – Full-bodied, robust, Indian.

CEYLON – Delicate and fragrant.

DARJEELING – The finest and most delicately flavored Indian tea. Grown in the Himalaya Mountains at high elevations.

EARL GREY – Aromatic and hearty flavor. From India and Ceylon.

ENGLISH BREAKFAST – A blend of black teas. Mellow and fragrant.

KEEMUN – Mild, robust. China congou type.

LAPSANG SOUCHONG – Unique, smoky flavor. Pungent and strong. Originally, a China tea. Now grown in Formosa.

SUMATRA – Usually used in blends with other teas. From the island of Sumatra in Indonesia, and Java.

Green

BASKET-FIRED – A Japanese tea, which makes a light, gentle brew.

GUNPOWDER – A delicate, pale tea from India, Ceylon, and Formosa. Each leaf is rolled in a pellet.

Oolong and Mixed

FORMOSA OOLONG—A semi-fermented tea with subtle flavor and aroma.

JASMINE—Delicately flavored with white jasmine blossoms.

HOT

HOT TEA

Pre-heat teapot with hot water. Bring fresh, cold tap-water to a full, rolling boil. Use 1 teaspoon of tea (or 1 tea bag) per cup. Brew 3 to 5 minutes depending on the strength you like.

TEA CONCENTRATE

This may be made hours before use and is The Answer to making good tea for many guests.

1½ quarts freshly drawn, cold water
¼ pound loose tea

Bring water to a full, rolling boil. Remove from heat and immediately add tea. Stir to immerse leaves. Cover. Brew 5 minutes. Strain into teapot or other container until ready to serve. Then into each cup pour 1 part concentrate to 7 parts boiling water. Yields about 40 to 45 servings.

HOT LEMON TEA

½ cup cold water
½ cup granulated sugar
1 quart boiling water
1½ tablespoons tea or 5
  tea bags

6 whole cloves
¼ cup lemon juice
6 slices lemon

Boil cold water and sugar in a saucepan. Reduce heat and simmer 10 minutes to make a simple syrup. Meanwhile, pour boiling water over tea. Brew 3 to 5 minutes. Strain into chafing dish, teapot, heat-resistant punch bowl, or samovar. Add syrup and lemon juice. To serve, place lemon slice speared with clove in each of 6 cups. Fill with tea.

PUNGENT HOT TEA

1 quart boiling water
2 tablespoons tea or 8 tea
  bags
¼ cup honey

¼ cup lemon juice
⅛ teaspoon Tabasco
6 slices lemon
6 cinnamon sticks

Pour boiling water over tea in heat-resistant pitcher. Add honey, lemon juice, and Tabasco. Stir. Serve hot in 6 mugs with a slice of lemon and cinnamon stick in each one.

MOROCCAN TEA

2 sprigs fresh mint, or
  1 heaping teaspoon
  dried mint
4 cups freshly boiled water

1 rounded teaspoon green
  tea
Sugar to taste

Put mint into teapot and pour over it only a few drops of boiled water. Pour this water out. Add tea and rest of water. Steep for about 5 minutes. Add sugar to taste. Yields about 4 cups.

ANISE TEA

1 teaspoon anise seeds
2 cups boiling water
2 cups hot tea

¼ cup chopped English
walnuts or pine nuts

Add anise seeds to boiling water in saucepan. Steep 10 minutes. Strain. Add liquid to tea. Serve in 4 delicate china cups. Garnish with chopped nuts.

RUSSIAN TEA

Serve with blini and sour cream.

1 cup hot tea
1 rounded teaspoon cherry or raspberry preserves

Serve in glass using holder or gloves*.

RUSSIAN HOLIDAY TEA

½ stick cinnamon
5 whole cloves
3 strips orange rind
3 cups water

3 teaspoons tea
Juice of ½ lemon
Juice of 1 orange
Lump sugar

Tie cinnamon and cloves in a cheesecloth bag. Drop bag and orange rind slices into water. Simmer on low flame for 10 minutes. Add tea, lemon juice, and orange juice. Steep for about 3 minutes. Strain into 4 cups. Serve with lump sugar.

* Joke.

HOT FRUIT TEA

¾ cup honey
6 cloves
1 short stick cinnamon
¼ teaspoon salt
1½ cups water
2½ cups pineapple juice

Juice of 2 lemons
2 cups strong, hot tea
12 maraschino cherries
with syrup
1 seedless orange, sliced
thin

Simmer honey, cloves, cinnamon, and salt in water for 5 minutes. Strain. Add juices and tea. Bring to a boil. Add cherries and sliced orange. Yields about 10 cups.

ENGLISH HOLIDAY HOT TEA PUNCH

5 quarts boiling water
½ cup loose tea or 12
tea bags
3 tablespoons whole
cloves
3 cups orange juice
1½ cups lemon juice

2 cups honey
Green and red maraschino
cherries
2 oranges, thinly sliced
Whole cloves
1 lemon, thinly sliced
12 short sticks cinnamon

Pour boiling water over the tea and the 3 tablespoons whole cloves. Steep in a covered container 5 minutes. Strain. Add fruit juices and honey. Stir until well blended. Keep warm (on very low heat). Pour into heat-resistant punch bowl. Stick red and green cherries in the orange slices with toothpicks. Stick several whole cloves into lemon slices. Garnish punch with the sliced fruit. Use cinnamon sticks as muddlers. Yields about 25 punch cups.

TISANES

These are herb teas; that is, teas brewed from herbs rather than from the dried tea plant.

HERB TEAS (PARTIAL LIST)

Alfalfa Leaf
Alfalfa Mint
Camomile
Desert Herb
Fenugreek Seed
Red Clover
Rose Hip
Shavegrass
Peppermint
Maté
Lindenblüten or Lime Blossom
Fennel Seed

Note: Many packaged herbs make teas as well: i.e., rosemary, tarragon, anise, saffron, etc.

TISANE FOR ONE

Approximately 1½ teaspoons herb tea
1 cup boiling water

Allow tea to steep in covered teapot for several minutes. Do not boil. Strain. Flavor with sugar or honey. Lemon or lime may be added.

COLD

ICED TEA

In the summer of 1904, at the Fair in St. Louis, crowds grew thickest where drinks were coldest. The Far East Teahouse took note, harmonized, and, for the first time in America, iced tea was heard from.

ICED TEA FOR ONE

Brew extra-strong tea in teapot about 6 minutes. Pour over ice cubes in 1 tall glass. Add cold water from tap. Serve with confectioners' sugar and lemon wedge.

Note: Instant powdered or liquid tea may be substituted for brewed tea.

ICED TEA FOR FIFTY

3 quarts boiling water   *2¼ gallons cold tap-water*
⅔ cup loose tea   *Ice cubes*

Pour boiling water over tea in a teapot. Brew about 6 minutes. Stir. Strain into large container with tap-water. Pour into tall glasses over ice cubes. Add lemon and sugar to taste. About 3 gallons.

Note: Refrigeration may cloud tea. A little hot water will clear it.

INSTANT ICED TEA

1 small jar instant tea
2½ quarts cold water
4 cans frozen lemonade, limeade, or orangeade concentrate
(do not dilute)

Put instant tea into a large pitcher. Add cold water. Stir thoroughly. Add frozen concentrate. Stir again. Yields about 1 gallon.

ICED TEA LEMONADE

¾ cup sugar
1 quart boiling water
⅓ cup loose tea or 15
  tea bags

1 quart cold water
¾ cup lemon juice
Ice cubes
8 slices lemon

Dissolve sugar in boiling water. Pour over loose tea. Brew 5 minutes. Stir. Strain into cold water. Add lemon juice. Serve in 8 tall glasses over ice cubes. Top with lemon slices.

LEMON FROSTED ICED TEA

⅓ cup loose tea or 15 tea bags
2 quarts cold water
1 quart lemon ice

Pre-measure tea. Bring 1 quart cold water to a full, rolling boil in a saucepan. Remove from heat, and immediately add all the tea at once. Stir. Brew 5 minutes, uncovered. Stir again. Strain into pitcher holding additional quart of cold water. Let cool at room temperature. Beat lemon ice with cooled tea until frothy. Pour into pitcher and serve immediately in 12 chilled glasses.

STRAWBERRY ICED TEA FIZZ

2½ cups boiling water
1 tablespoon tea leaves
  (black or oolong)
1 ten-ounce package frozen
  strawberries, thawed

1 six-ounce can frozen
  limeade concentrate,
  thawed
2 cups club soda, chilled
Ice cubes

Pour boiling water over tea. Let steep 5 minutes. Stir, then strain. Let cool at room temperature. Add strawberries and limeade concentrate. Chill. Add club soda and serve immediately in tall glasses (10-ounce) with ice cubes. Serves 6 to 8.

FRUIT-TEA SWIZZLE

2 quarts cold water
⅓ cup loose tea or 15
  tea bags
3 tablespoons lime juice
3 tablespoons lemon juice

Sugar (optional)
Ice cubes
Fruit swizzle sticks (see
  Herbs and Garnishes)

Bring 1 quart cold water to a full, rolling boil in a saucepan. Remove from heat. While water is still bubbling, add all the tea at once. Stir. Brew 5 minutes, uncovered. Stir again. Strain into pitcher holding the additional quart of cold water. Add fruit juices and sugar. Do not refrigerate. Serve in tall glasses with ice cubes. Add fruit swizzle stick to each glass. Yields about 10 glasses.

APRICOT TEA PUNCH

5 cups water
⅓ cup loose tea or 15
   tea bags
1 tablespoon nutmeg
1 cup superfine sugar

6 cups apricot nectar
1 cup lemon juice
Ice block
1 quart chilled club soda

Bring water to a boil in a saucepan. Remove from heat. Immediately add tea and nutmeg. Brew 4 minutes. Stir, then cool. Strain into punch bowl containing sugar and fruit juices. Stir again. When ready to serve, add block of ice and club soda. Yields about 30 punch cups.

CAPE COD TEA PUNCH

1 quart water
2 heaping tablespoons
   loose tea or 7 tea bags
½ teaspoon nutmeg
½ teaspoon cinnamon
½ teaspoon allspice
1½ cups superfine sugar

1 cup orange juice
½ cup lemon juice
1 quart chilled cranberry
   juice cocktail
Ice cubes
1 quart chilled club soda

Bring water to a boil in a saucepan. Remove from heat. Immediately add tea, nutmeg, cinnamon, and allspice. Brew 4 minutes. Stir. Strain into a punch bowl containing sugar and orange, lemon, and cranberry juices. Just before serving add ice cubes and club soda. Yields about 40 punch cups.

WAIKIKI PUNCH

2 quarts tea (freshly
brewed and cooled)
1 large can diced
pineapple
12 cups orange juice
2 cups lemon juice

1 small bottle maraschino
cherries
3 large bottles pale dry
ginger ale
Sugar syrup to taste
Ice block

Stir all other ingredients before adding sugar syrup. Serve over
ice block in punch bowl. Yields about 50 punch cups.

(Other) Hot Shots

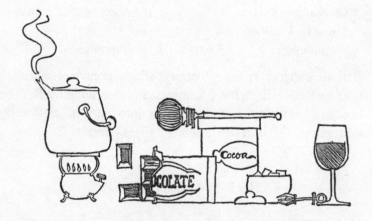

I refuse to say something cozy about hot drinks and their automatic hookup with snuggling, crackling fires, et al. Hot drinks, like most other nice things, are for whenever you feel like it—and that may be during a sore throat in July, or a bubble bath in August.

What matters is: (1) to know that other hot drinks exist, and (2) not to get so wedged in the coffee/tea slot that you forget that they exist. There are times when coffee and tea, no matter what you do to them, aren't enough *fun*. This chapter is for those times—whenever they are.

HOT FRUIT DRINK

2 cups orange juice	1 teaspoon whole cloves
¼ cup sugar	1 teaspoon grated lemon
3 one-inch sticks	peel
cinnamon	4 slices orange

Boil all ingredients except orange slices in enamel saucepan over moderate heat for 1 minute. Stir occasionally. Reduce heat and simmer 5 minutes. Strain into pitcher, or directly into mugs. Garnish with orange slices. Serves 4.

HOT MULLED CIDER

I

3 quarts cider	½ teaspoon nutmeg
1 teaspoon whole cloves	Several short sticks
⅓ cup sugar	cinnamon

Boil all ingredients for 5 minutes. Strain into pitcher or directly into mugs. Serves about 12.

HOT MULLED CIDER

II

1 cup brown sugar, loosely packed	3 sticks cinnamon
Pinch salt	Pinch nutmeg
1 teaspoon allspice	2 quarts cider

Add sugar, salt, and spices to cider. Simmer slowly for about 10 minutes. Strain. Serve hot in 8 mugs.

CALIFORNIA CIDER

5 cups boiling water
2 tea bags
5 cups apple cider
1¼ cups brown sugar
1 stick cinnamon, crushed
⅛ teaspoon ground nutmeg or mace
⅛ teaspoon ground allspice

3 cups fresh orange juice
1 cup fresh lemon juice
Green and red maraschino cherries
1 unpeeled lemon, sliced thin
1 unpeeled California orange, sliced thin

Pour boiling water over tea bags. Let steep for 5 minutes. Meanwhile, combine cider, sugar, cinnamon, nutmeg, and allspice in saucepan and bring to a boil. Reduce heat, and simmer for about 4 minutes. Add orange and lemon juices, and hot tea. Heat, but do not boil. With wooden toothpicks, fasten red cherries to lemon slices, and green cherries to orange slices. Pour hot punch into heat-resistant punch bowl. Garnish with fruit slices. About 1 gallon.

HOT DR. PEPPER

1 cup Dr. Pepper or other fruit-flavored bottled soda
Wedge of lemon

Heat soda. Squeeze part of lemon into 1 mug. Add soda. Squeeze remaining lemon, and serve steaming.

TARTAR'S TEA

Serve with small balls of steak tartare fastened with toothpicks
to thinly sliced radishes.

1 cup bottled borscht
(use liquid only)
1 cup canned beef
bouillon or beef
consommé
1 cup tomato juice
1 cup sauerkraut juice

½ cup carrot juice (for
thicker, creamier flavor;
optional)
Coarsely ground black
pepper to taste
Fresh or dried dill leaves

Heat all liquids. Add pepper. Serve steaming in 5 small mugs.
Garnish with dill.

INDONESIAN GINGER

I

Pungent, spicy, and sweet.

3 slices ginger
⅓ cup brown sugar
2 cups water

Simmer all ingredients about ½ hour. Serve very hot in 2 cups.

INDONESIAN GINGER

II

¼ cup ginger syrup*
½ cup lime juice
Hot water

2 pieces preserved ginger,
cut small

* See JAIPUR GINGER in Extracts, Essences, Etceteras.

Mix syrup and lime juice. Pour into 2 mugs. Fill with hot water. Garnish with ginger.

SYRIAN DRINK

Serve with sesame-seed crackers and jam.

2 cups water	1 teaspoon anise seeds
1 stick cinnamon	Sugar to taste
1 whole clove	2 almonds or walnuts
2 slices ginger	

Boil water with spices until mixture turns dark. Add sugar. Pour into 2 cups. Garnish each with almond or walnut.

HOT FINNISH FRUIT PUNCH

5 lemons	2 tablespoons sugar
1 pint sweetened cherry	1 pint water
juice	2 bottles club soda

Squeeze 3 lemons, and mix juice with cherry juice. Heat sugar and water until a very light syrup is formed. Add lemon-cherry juice. Slice remaining 2 lemons. Just before serving, put lemon slices and club soda into heat-resistant punch bowl. Add boiling syrup. Serve hot. Yields about 12 cups.

RUSSIAN RASPBERRIES

Use glasses with holders if available.

I

Like RUSSIAN TEA, this drink is traditionally served in a glass.

¼ cup raspberry jam	1 tablespoon lemon juice
¾ cup boiling water	Slice of lemon

Stir jam in water. Bring to a boil and add lemon juice. Serve in 1 glass with lemon slice.

RUSSIAN RASPBERRIES

II

2 tablespoons fresh lemon juice	1 teaspoon powdered sugar
1 tablespoon raspberry juice	Boiling water

Stir together lemon juice, raspberry juice, and sugar. Pour into 1 glass. Fill with boiling water.

RUSSIAN RASPBERRIES

III

1 tablespoon dried raspberries
1 cup boiling water
Sugar to taste

Steep raspberries in water 3 minutes. Pour liquid and berries into 1 glass. Add sugar.

HOT JAMAICA PUNCH

1 *cup molasses*
2 *tablespoons ginger syrup**
2 *tablespoons sugar*

2 *tablespoons cream*
Grated rind of ½ lemon
1 *quart hot milk*
Grated nutmeg

Stir all ingredients, except nutmeg, into hot milk. Pour into 6 mugs. Sprinkle nutmeg on top of each.

DUTCH SAGE MILK

This is good cold, too.

1 *cup milk*
1 *teaspoon sugar*
¼ *teaspoon powdered, dried sage*

Heat milk to boiling point. Add sugar and sage. Stir. Serve in 1 cup or mug.

MILK ANISE

Serve with butter cookies.

1¾ *cups milk*
1 *teaspoon crushed anise seeds*

¼ *cup sugar (or less)*
2 *teaspoons cornstarch*

Scald milk and anise seeds. Add sugar and simmer 5 minutes. Dissolve cornstarch in a little water. Add to mixture. Stir and let simmer 5 minutes more. Serve in 2 mugs.

* See JAIPUR GINGER in *Extracts, Essences, Etceteras.*

DUTCH CHRISTMAS DRINK

1 small piece of stick cinnamon	1 small piece ginger root
4 cloves	2 cups milk
Pinch saffron	¼ cup sugar
1 small piece mace	3 teaspoons cornstarch
	⅛ cup cold water

Put herbs and spices in individual aluminum tea brewer, or tie together in small muslin bag. Immerse in milk, and bring to boil. Turn flame down immediately, then simmer 15 minutes. Add sugar. Dissolve cornstarch in water. Add to hot milk. Simmer again for 5 minutes. Remove herb bag. Serve hot in 2 mugs.

CHILDREN'S CUSTARD DRINK

4 cups milk	⅓ cup dark brown sugar
4 beaten eggs	Ground nutmeg

Heat milk in double boiler. Slowly add to beaten eggs. Stir constantly. Put egg-and-milk mixture back into double boiler. Heat again, and keep stirring. Add brown sugar. Stir. Pour into 8 cups. Sprinkle each drink with nutmeg.

DIXIE ALMOND

¾ cup blanched almonds	1 tablespoon rose water
1 stick cinnamon	Sugar to taste
4 cups milk	

Crush almonds and cinnamon stick in a mortar. (May be put through food mill or blended.) Add to milk. Add rose water and sugar. Bring to a boiling point. Strain. Serve hot in 4 cups.

HOT COCOA

1 tablespoon cocoa   ¼ cup water
2 teaspoons sugar   ¾ cup milk
Dash salt

Mix cocoa, sugar, salt, and water. Boil gently for 2 minutes, stirring constantly. Add milk. Heat, but do not boil. Makes 1 cup.

EASY HOT CHOCOLATE

1 square bitter chocolate   ⅓ cup hot milk
3 tablespoons sugar   Whipped cream
⅓ cup water

Put chocolate, sugar, and water in top of double boiler. Cook over boiling water for about 10 minutes, stirring frequently. Add hot milk. Stir again. Garnish with whipped cream. Makes 2 chocolate cups.

HOT CHOCOLATE EXCELSIOR

2 squares unsweetened
  chocolate
1 cup water
3 tablespoons sugar
Pinch salt
3 cups milk
Grated orange rind

¼ teaspoon almond
  extract
¼ teaspoon vanilla extract
6 rounded teaspoons
  whipped cream
6 swirls orange rind

Melt chocolate in water in top of double boiler. Keep flame low, and stir constantly. Add sugar and salt. Simmer 3 minutes, stirring constantly. Add milk gradually. Stir in orange rind, almond and vanilla extracts. Heat. Remove from flame and beat until frothy. Pour into 6 chocolate cups. Add spoonful of whipped cream to each cup. Top with orange rind.

CHERRY CHOCOLATE FOR CHILDREN

This is pretty gooey.

6 tablespoons chocolate
  syrup
4 cups milk
½ cup regular-sized
  marshmallows

18 miniature marshmallows
12 maraschino cherries

Mix chocolate syrup with milk. Add ½ cup marshmallows. Heat. Stir occasionally, until marshmallows dissolve. Put 3 miniature marshmallows and 2 cherries alternately on each of 6 toothpicks. Pour hot chocolate mixture into 6 cups. Garnish with cherry-marshmallow kebob.

MEXICAN HOT CHOCOLATE

2 cups milk
2 ounces sweet cooking
  chocolate, broken up

2 small sticks cinnamon
2 egg whites, stiffly beaten

Heat 1 cup of the milk; add chocolate and heat and stir over low heat until chocolate is melted. Add remaining milk and cinnamon sticks. Bring to boiling point. Remove from heat. Remove cinnamon and beat with a rotary beater or wire whisk until smooth. Gradually add beaten egg whites. Continue to beat mixture until frothy. Serve in chocolate cups. Serves 3.

DUTCH MOCHA

2 squares unsweetened
  chocolate, broken up
6 tablespoons sugar
3 cups milk
¼ teaspoon salt

3 cups strong, hot coffee
8 rounded teaspoons
  whipped cream
Nutmeg

Cook chocolate, sugar, and 1½ cups of the milk in double boiler until chocolate is dissolved. Stir. Add salt and remaining milk. Continue cooking until mixture is hot. Beat, adding coffee slowly, until frothy. Pour into 8 chocolate cups. Top each with whipped cream and dash of nutmeg.

HOT MOLASSES AND MILK

1 tablespoon molasses   *½ cup boiling water*
½ teaspoon ginger   *½ cup hot milk*

Mix molasses with ginger in saucepan. Pour boiling water over mixture and continue to boil for 1 minute. Add milk. Serve in 1 mug.

Note: Other hot drinks in *Bogus Booze*.

Mostly Milk

Milk will never pass for Scotch and soda. Like baseball, like red balloons, like Betty Grable movies in the forties, *milk*, the most nutritious of the non-drinks, is sublimely square. That, in five more than twenty-five words and no box top, is why I love milk.

Which is not to say that milk shouldn't be fiddled with. There is a plethora of reasons for fiddling with milk: the most obvious is that a child who dislikes milk may lap it up like the cat next door if syrup or fruit is thrown in, or if, through blender magic, a soda-fountain drink is approximated.

Fiddling with skim milk is especially gratifying. To begin with something akin to white water and, having maintained the same calorie and cholesterol count, wind up with something that Dolley Madison would have served her husband on election day is a triumph for any forward-thinking non-drinker.

Drinks made from yoghurt (I stop at nothing) shoot the square theory (see above) sky high.

FRUIT MILK

⅔ *cup milk*
⅓ *cup of one of the following:*
  canned or crushed pineapple
  canned or frozen peaches
  sweetened fresh or frozen strawberries, raspberries, or
    cherries

Beat ingredients, or blend for about 15 seconds. Serve cold in 1 glass.

BANANA WHIP (B)

1 *cup milk*	*About 1 cup crushed ice*
1 *banana, cut up*	*Sugar* (*optional*)

Blend all ingredients until mixture is thick and blender container is almost full. Pour into 2 tall glasses.

FRUIT FRAPPE (B)

A nutritious dessert drink.

1 *cup milk*	2 *teaspoons honey*
1 *banana*	⅛ *teaspoon almond*
1 *orange, peeled and cut*	*extract*
into small pieces	*Pinch salt*
1 *strip orange rind*	

Blend all ingredients first on low speed, then on high. When fruits are entirely liquefied, pour into freezing tray. Freeze partially. Spoon immediately into 2 parfait glasses and serve with small spoons or short straws.

CARROT MILK BLEND

About 6 thin slices	½ *cup chilled, canned*
banana	*carrot juice*
½ *cup cold milk*	1 *teaspoon honey*

Mash banana. Add other ingredients and beat. Or blend all ingredients.

ST. THOMAS CHOCOLATE

2 *cups chilled, bottled*	*Angostura bitters*
chocolate milk	2 *twelve-ounce bottles or*
½ *cup heavy cream*	*cans cold cream soda*

In each of 4 glasses (8-ounce) pour ½ cup of milk, 2 tablespoons cream, and a dash of bitters. Stir. Fill each glass with cream soda. Stir gently. Serve immediately. Serves 4.

Note: For similar drinks, see Egg Creams in *Syrups.*

APRES SCHOOL COCKTAIL

1 cup cold milk   ¼ teaspoon vanilla extract
2 tablespoons maple syrup   Dash salt

Blend, beat, or stir all ingredients. Serve in 1 tall glass.

CINNAMON CHOCOLATE

8 tablespoons chocolate   ¼ cup whipped cream
   syrup   ⅛ teaspoon cinnamon
4 cups milk

Mix chocolate syrup with milk. Pour into 4 glasses. Top with whipped cream and cinnamon.

PEANUT BUTTER MILK

I

The sign reads, "For Children Only." It may be ignored.

¼ cup honey
¼ cup creamy peanut butter
3½ cups cold milk

Beat honey and peanut butter until well blended. Gradually add ½ cup of milk. Beat until smooth. Pour in remaining milk. Beat again, or blend all ingredients. Yields 4 glasses.

PEANUT BUTTER MILK

II

4 *tablespoons chocolate syrup*
2 *cups cold milk*
2 *tablespoons creamy peanut butter*

Mix chocolate syrup in milk. Put peanut butter into mixing
bowl and add chocolate milk very slowly, stirring constantly,
until blended. Or blend all ingredients. Makes 2 glasses.

ALMOND FOAM

2 *tablespoons orgeat syrup* 1 *beaten egg white*
3 *tablespoons sweet cream* ¾ *cup cold milk*
Powdered sugar to taste

Beat syrup, sweet cream, and sugar lightly. Pour into 1 glass.
Add beaten egg white and fill with milk. Stir briefly.

ALMOND FLIP

2 *tablespoons orgeat syrup* ¼ *cup cracked ice*
1 *tablespoon plain sugar* ¾ *cup milk*
  *syrup**

Mix together syrups and cracked ice in 1 tall glass. Fill with
milk. Stir.

* See TEA TONIC in *The Other Standards*.

VEGETABLE MILK (JE)

4 carrots, cut up
½ large stalk celery (with leaves), cut up
1 cup milk

Put carrots and celery through juice extractor. Divide liquid
into 2 glasses. Fill with milk. Stir.

ALL-DAY DIET (B)

930 calories.

1¼ cup evaporated milk   2 tablespoons corn oil
1 cup pineapple juice   ½ cup brewers' yeast
⅓ cup dextrose

Blend on high speed for 20 seconds. Chill. Drink 4 ounces
5 times daily. Makes 5 portions.

EGGNOGS

A thick drink made of beaten eggs, milk, sugar, and flavoring, served in a punch (or nog) cup—that is an eggnog.
Specifically:

SIMPLE EGGNOG

½ pint milk or ¼ pint   1 teaspoon sugar
   milk and ¼ pint sweet   ⅛ teaspoon vanilla
   cream   Nutmeg
1 egg

Beat or blend milk, egg, sugar, and vanilla for a few seconds. Serve in 4 punch cups. Sprinkle nutmeg on top of each.

HOLIDAY EGGNOG

4 eggs, separated	1 cup whipped cream
¼ teaspoon salt	½ teaspoon vanilla
½ cup sugar	Grated nutmeg
3 cups milk	

Beat egg yolks. Gradually add salt and half the sugar. Continue to beat. Add milk and cream gradually. Cook mixture in double boiler, stirring constantly, until it is thick enough to coat a silver spoon. Cool. Add vanilla. Chill thoroughly. Beat egg whites to soft peaks, while gradually pouring in the remaining sugar. Beat the chilled custard (first mixture) until smooth and frothy. Fold in beaten egg whites. Sprinkle nutmeg on top. Serve in 16 punch cups.

Note: The sugar may be decreased by 2 tablespoons and supplemented instead by ¼ cup cinnamon or peppermint candies added to the mixture before cooking.

CIDER EGGNOG

Cracked ice makes a thicker nog.

1 egg	¼ cup cracked ice
1 teaspoon confectioners' sugar	1 cup sweet cider
	Freshly grated nutmeg
½ cup milk	

Combine egg, sugar, milk, and ice and blend in an electric blender until smooth. Add cider. Mix well. Serve in punch cups. Sprinkle nutmeg on top. Serves 4.

CRANBERRY NOG

½ cup sweet cream   2 teaspoons sugar
½ cup cranberry juice   ½ cup cracked ice
1 egg

Beat or blend until thick. Serve immediately in 5 punch cups.

APRICOT NOG

½ cup apricot nectar   ½ cup cracked ice
½ cup sweet cream   Grated nutmeg
1 egg

Beat or blend all ingredients, except nutmeg, until thick.
Serve immediately in 5 punch cups. Sprinkle nutmeg on top.

BANANA NOG

½ ripe banana, cut up   1 teaspoon vanilla
1 cup milk   ½ cup crushed ice
1 egg   Grated nutmeg

Mash banana. Add other ingredients, except nutmeg. Beat or
blend until thick. Serve in 5 punch cups. Sprinkle nutmeg on
top.

Note: Eggnogs made with skim milk in following section.

SKIM MILK

Most of the ingredients accompanying skim milk in this section are equally bereft of caloric content.

GRAND ILLUSION (B) (D)

I

Has everything but calories.

1 *glass skim milk*   *Non-caloric liquid substitute*
1 *cup crushed ice*   *for 2 teaspoons sugar*
2 *tablespoons strawberries*
  or raspberries

Blend all ingredients on high speed until frothy. Pour into 2 very tall glasses.

GRAND ILLUSION (B) (D)

II

1 *glass skim milk*
1 *cup crushed ice*
3 *tablespoons low-calorie syrup*

Follow directions for GRAND ILLUSION I.

HAWAIIAN MILK SHAKE (D)

1 *cup unsweetened pineapple juice*
3½ *cups skim milk*
4 *medium chunks of pineapple*

Mix pineapple juice and skim milk. Chill. Serve in 4 glasses.
Garnish with pineapple chunks.

PEACH MILK (B) (D)

¼ *cup cut-up canned*   ½ *cup liquid skim milk*
   peaches   *Sugar substitute to taste*
¼ *cup crushed ice*   1 *sprig mint*

Blend all ingredients, except mint, in an electric blender until
foamy. Garnish with mint. Makes 1 8-ounce glass.

ORANGE MILK (D)

½ *cup orange juice*   1 *egg*
½ *cup cold skim milk*   ⅛ *teaspoon salt*
Sugar substitute to taste

Beat, or blend all ingredients on high speed, for 10 seconds.
Serve in 1 tall glass.

STRAWBERRY RENNET DRINK

I

1½ cups chilled skim milk
⅓ cup orange juice
1½ tablespoons strawberry rennet dessert powder

Beat or blend until frothy. Yields 2 glasses.

STRAWBERRY RENNET DRINK

II

2 tablespoons dietetic fruit-flavored jelly
1¾ cups skim milk
1 tablespoon strawberry rennet dessert powder

Break currant jelly with a fork. Add to milk and beat. Add rennet powder. Beat again. Serve cold in 2 glasses.

BLENDER BREAKFAST (B) (D)

½ cup grapefruit juice   ½ cup dry cereal
½ cup cold skim milk   1 teaspoon brown sugar

Blend for about ½ minute. Serve in 2 juice glasses.

LIME EGGNOG (D)

1 small egg, separated
Dash salt
3 tablespoons fresh lime
    juice

Non-caloric liquid
    substitute for 6 teaspoons
    sugar
1¼ cups skim milk

Beat egg yolk. Add salt. Mix most of the lime juice with most of the liquid sweetener. Add to beaten yolk. Beat until fluffy. Stir in milk. Chill. Beat egg white until soft peaks form. Add remaining lime juice and liquid sweetener. Beat until peaks are stiff, but not dry. Fold half of egg-white mixture into yolk mixture. Serve in 5 chilled punch cups. Top each drink with remaining egg-white mixture.

VITA EGGNOG (B)

440 calories.

1 egg
½ cup skim milk
    or
1 tablespoon brewers'
    yeast and ½ cup
    non-fat dry milk solids

¾ cup apple juice

Blend on high speed for about 10 seconds. Serve in 2 punch cups.

Note: Eggnogs made with whole milk in preceding section.

BUTTERMILK

Like skim milk, buttermilk is very low in fat (5%).

STRAWBERRY BUTTERMILK

¾ cup sweetened, fresh strawberries
1½ cups cold buttermilk

Mash strawberries. Mix with buttermilk in 1 tall glass.

APRICOT BUTTERMILK BREEZE

1 cup cold buttermilk
1 cup apricot nectar
Sugar to taste

Mix. Serve very cold in 2 glasses.

PINEAPPLE BUTTERMILK

I

⅔ cup cold buttermilk
⅓ cup cold pineapple juice

Mix. Serve in 1 tall glass.

PINEAPPLE BUTTERMILK

II

¾ cup cold buttermilk   2 tablespoons sugar
¼ cup pineapple juice   1 tablespoon lemon juice

Mix. Serve cold in 1 tall glass.

BUTTERMILK BRUNCH (B)

1 cup cold buttermilk
2 chilled stewed prunes
1 tablespoon cold prune juice

Blend and serve in 1 large glass.

SPICE APPLE BUTTERMILK

4 cups cold buttermilk   Sugar to taste (about
2 cups chilled applesauce   4 teaspoons)
1 tablespoon lemon juice   Ground cinnamon

Mix buttermilk, applesauce, and lemon juice. Add sugar. Serve
in mugs. Sprinkle cinnamon on top. Serves 6.

BUTTERMILK FRUIT WHIRL

1 medium banana   6 tablespoons sugar
1 teaspoon lemon juice   6 cups cold buttermilk
½ cup crushed raspberries

Mash banana. Add lemon juice, raspberries, and sugar. Mix well. Chill in refrigerator ½ hour. Stir into buttermilk. Serve in 8 tall glasses.

FARMER'S MARKET

I

A pink drink with bite.

½ cup canned
vegetable juice
½ cup cold buttermilk

Dash Tabasco
Dash salt
Dash Worcestershire sauce

Mix all ingredients. Serve very cold in 1 glass.

FARMER'S MARKET

II

½ cup tomato juice
½ cup cold buttermilk

Dash curry
Dash salt

Mix. Serve very cold in 1 glass.

VANILLA BUTTERMILK FIZZ

½ cup cold buttermilk
½ cup cold cream soda
Dash powdered nutmeg

Stir buttermilk and soda gently. Serve immediately in 1 glass. Garnish with nutmeg.

CHERRY BUTTERMILK FIZZ

½ cup cold buttermilk
¾ cup cold black cherry soda

Stir. Serve immediately in 1 tall glass.

*   *   *

YOGHURT

Yoghurt, which begins as pasteurized milk and, after a few hours of controlled fermentation (in an incubator), turns into *The* nutritious milk food*, can become, with an added spurt of courage and effort, *The* nutritious milk-food-*drink*. (Probably no one, by the way, except the presidents of other yoghurt companies and their families, doubts that Dannon is *The* yoghurt company.)

FRUIT YOGHURT (B)

1 cup plain yoghurt
½ package frozen fruit

Blend until foamy. Serve immediately in 2 tall glasses.

* In most yoghurt, 50% of the butterfat is removed; proteins, minerals, vitamins, and cultures are added.

BANANA YOGHURT SWIRL (B)

1 *cup vanilla yoghurt*
1 *small banana*
1 *teaspoon sugar*

Blend. Yields about 2 tall glasses.

YOGHURT RASPBERRY SODA (D)

½ *cup chilled raspberry yoghurt*
1 *sixteen-ounce bottle low-calorie raspberry soda*

Mix. Serve very cold in 2 glasses.

VEGETARIAN LIQUID LUNCHEON (B) (D)

600 calories.

1 *cup chilled plain yoghurt*	2 *tablespoons brewers' yeast*
¼ *cup non-fat dry milk solids*	1 *egg*
½ *cup grape juice*	1 *tablespoon plain gelatin*

Blend all ingredients on high speed for 10 seconds. Yields about 2 cups.

CLAM YOGHURT COCKTAIL (B)

Serve before a cold crabmeat or lobster-salad lunch.

1 *container chilled plain yoghurt*
1 *cup clam juice*

Blend until foamy. Serve cold in 4 cocktail glasses.

BOMBAY COOLER

½ *small lime*
1 *cup yoghurt*
1⅓ *cups water*
1 *teaspoon chili powder*

½ *teaspoon sugar*
1 *rounded teaspoon dried,*
crushed mint
Salt to taste

Squeeze lime. Shake or mix juice and rind with all other ingredients. Refrigerate until cold (about 1 hour). Strain, pressing leaves with spoon to get maximum flavor. Serve in 4 cocktail glasses.

From the Fountain (Yours)

You don't have to be Howard Johnson to make an egg cream. Or even an ice cream soda. All you need are the ingredients, the equipment*, a nine-year-old on Saturday afternoon who won't settle for milk (on Saturday afternoon a kid deserves a break), or the kind of forty-five-year-old who still goes to the zoo.

The advantage of do-it-yourself Fountain Wonders is that you get what you want *exactly*—with not much trouble, really. Twenty-eight flavors or no, the aforementioned Mr. Johnson isn't about to squirt almond extract in anyone's cherry nut soda. And even good old moderation-in-all-things Schrafft's has yet to serve a chocolate ice cream soda that has 125 calories.**

* Soda glasses, straws, long spoons, and an ice cream scoop. (A blender is necessary for some fountain drinks, but not for sodas.)
** See DIETER'S INSTANT ICE CREAM SODA.

I won't say a thing about getting to be the most popular mother on the block which may, understandably, lead you to bury the ice cream scoop in the family plot—and me along with it.

ICE CREAM SODA

2 *tablespoons syrup*
2 *tablespoons milk*
1 *large scoop ice cream*

Carbonated water
Dash whipped cream

Put syrup, milk, and ice cream in 1 soda glass. Add carbonated water very gradually.* Stir. Garnish with whipped cream.

DIETER'S INSTANT ICE CREAM SODA (D)

About 125 calories.

Low-calorie soda (or 2
tablespoons low-calorie
syrup and carbonated
water)

2 tablespoons skim milk
1 scoop ice milk
Low-calorie synthetic
whipped cream

Follow directions for ICE CREAM SODA.

* At professional fountains a fizzier soda is achieved by reversing the handle of the soda tap, thereby increasing the pressure of the flow of soda. To get the maximum pressure when pouring carbonated soda from a bottle, cap the opening with your thumb and turn the bottle down at an angle, allowing the soda to squirt into the glass. Or, of course, a siphon may be used, which is a modern version of the old seltzer bottle.

SOME USUAL AND UNUSUAL
ICE CREAM SODA COMBINATIONS

Follow ICE CREAM SODA directions.

BLACK AND WHITE

Chocolate syrup*
Vanilla ice cream

HOBOKEN

Pineapple syrup
Chocolate ice cream

CHOCOLATE CHIP COFFEE

Coffee syrup
Chocolate chip ice cream

APRICOT MINT

Apricot syrup
Mint chocolate chip ice cream

* Chocolate syrup recipe in syrup section.

CHERRY NUT

Cherry syrup
Burnt almond ice cream
Dash almond extract

CONEY ISLAND

Root beer syrup
Vanilla ice cream

Omit milk in making soda.

FRESH PEACH

Fresh peach syrup
Peach ice cream

Note: Generally, it's open season in choosing flavors for ice cream sodas and floats (where the ice cream is left intact). Otherwise, in frosteds, milk shakes, and malteds, it is best to choose syrups and ice creams that are the same – or that are highly compatible, i.e.:
    chocolate and coffee
    one fruit flavor and another
    vanilla and almost any other flavor.

*   *   *

FROSTED (B)

In a frosted the ice cream's *almost* melted.

2 ounces syrup
1 cup milk
1 scoop ice cream

Blend for at least 30 seconds. Serve in 2 soda glasses.

MILK SHAKE (B)

The old-fashioned milk shake was made like a frosted, but without ice cream. Now, usually ice cream *is* used, but it is thoroughly dissolved in the mixture.

FLOAT

Same as FROSTED, with extra scoop of ice cream added to glass before serving.

MALTED MILK (B)

2 ounces syrup   *1 teaspoon powdered,*
1 scoop ice cream   *unflavored malt*
½ pint milk

Blend on high speed for about 1½ minutes, or until mixture is thick and there is about twice the original amount. Serve in 2 soda glasses.

VIENNESE VELVET

1 *pint vanilla ice cream*   *Whipped cream*
3 *cups hot,*   *Shaved chocolate or*
   double-strength coffee   *grated orange peel*
Nutmeg

Put one scoop of the ice cream into each of 6 glasses. Pour hot coffee over ice cream until each glass is ⅔ full. Add second scoop ice cream. Sprinkle with nutmeg. Fill glasses with more hot coffee. Top with rounded teaspoon whipped cream, and shaved chocolate or grated orange peel.

MOCHA FROTH (B)

4 *teaspoons chocolate*   1 *teaspoon sugar*
   syrup   ¾ *cup milk*
1 *scoop coffee ice cream*
1½ *teaspoons instant*
   coffee

Blend syrup, ice cream, coffee, and sugar on high speed. With motor running on low speed, add milk gradually. Serve in 1 tall glass.

MAPLE FIZZ

2 *tablespoons maple syrup*   1 *scoop maple or butter*
4 *tablespoons sweet cream*   *pecan ice cream*
½ *glass cracked ice*   *Carbonated water*

Pour syrup, cream, and ice into shaker. Shake well. Transfer drink to 1 tall glass. Add ice cream. Gradually fill glass with carbonated water.

CURRANT CREAM COOLER

For the grownups.

¾ cup sugar	3½ cups water
3 cups fresh red currants	2 cups vanilla ice cream

Cook sugar, currants, and 1 cup water in a saucepan, stirring occasionally, for about 5 minutes or until currants are soft. Press through a sieve. Add remaining 2½ cups water. Chill. Put ice cream in 6 glasses and fill with currant juice.

BANANA CREAM (B)

1 sliced banana
1 cup milk
1 scoop banana ice cream

Blend banana and milk until smooth. Add ice cream. Blend again until ice cream is melted. Serve immediately in 1 very tall glass.

Note: Other matched fruit and ice cream flavors may be substituted, i.e., peach, strawberry, pineapple.

PEACHES-AND-CREAM FROSTED (B)

½ cup chilled peaches   Pinch salt
½ cup milk   ½ cup vanilla ice cream
3 drops almond extract

Blend all ingredients, except ice cream, on high speed. Add ice cream and blend until it is almost, but not entirely, liquefied. Serve immediately in 3 glasses.

MELON CREAM SHAKE (B)

1 ripe medium cantaloupe,   2 tablespoons lemon juice
   peeled, seeded, and cut   2 tablespoons sugar
   up   1 pint vanilla ice cream
½ cup milk

Blend all ingredients, except ice cream, on high speed for 10 seconds. Add ice cream. Blend again until mixture is smooth. Serve in 4 tall glasses.

CITRUS CREAM (B)

1½ cups sweetened   ¼ cup confectioners'
   pineapple juice   sugar
Juice of 1 lime   1 pint softened vanilla ice
1 strip lime peel   cream

Combine pineapple juice, lime juice, lime peel, and sugar. Blend in an electric blender on high speed for about 10 seconds. Add ice cream. Blend until smooth. Serve in tall glasses (10-ounce). Serves 4.

APPLE CREAM

1 *cup soft vanilla ice cream*
1 *pint apple juice*
Grated *nutmeg*

Beat or blend ice cream and apple juice. Serve in 3 tall glasses and garnish with nutmeg.

GINGER SMOOTHIE

¾ *cup ginger ale*
1 *scoop soft vanilla ice cream*
1 *tablespoon crushed, canned pineapple, with juice*

Beat or blend. Serve in 1 tall glass.

SHERBETS AND ICES

The main difference between the two is that sherbet is made with milk. Both are a gay addition to summer drinks. The best sweet ones and those which include club soda may be accompanied by wedges of fruit.

ORANGE FREEZE (B)

1 *cup orange juice*
1 *scoop orange sherbet* (or *vanilla ice cream*)

Blend until frothy. Serve in 1 tall glass.

ORANGE FREEZE FLOAT

4 mint leaves
1 cup chilled orange juice
1 pint orange sherbet

Crush mint leaves in pitcher. Add juice. Refrigerate for about 1 hour. Strain to remove mint leaves. Pour into 6 chilled glasses and add a scoop of sherbet to each glass.

FRUIT FLOAT

1 cup orange juice
1 cup unsweetened
  pineapple juice
⅛ cup lemon juice

½ pint pineapple or
  orange sherbet
3 sprigs mint

Combine juices. Chill. Scoop sherbet into 3 tall glasses. Fill with juice mixture. Garnish with mint.

GINGER MIST

1 cup cold ginger ale
1 scoop lemon sherbet

Maraschino cherry
Sprig of fresh mint

Pour ginger ale into 1 soda glass. Add scoop of sherbet on top. Garnish with cherry and mint.

LEMON ORANGE FIZZ (B)

Juice of 1 orange   Ice cubes
½ scoop lemon sherbet   Ginger ale

Blend orange juice and sherbet. Pour over ice cubes in 1 tall
glass. Add ginger ale. Stir gently and serve immediately.

NECTAR FROST

½ cup apricot nectar
1 scoop soft lemon sherbet
2 drops mint extract

Beat or blend. Serve in 1 tall glass.

RASPBERRY LEMONADE

I

1 can frozen lemonade concentrate
Water
1 pint raspberry sherbet

Combine lemonade and water, as directed on can. Pour into
4 tall glasses. Add 1 scoop of sherbet to each glass.

RASPBERRY LEMONADE

II

1 *can frozen lemonade*   1 *pint raspberry sherbet*
concentrate   *Club soda*
Water

Combine lemonade and water as directed on can. Pour into 6 tall glasses. Add 1 scoop of sherbet to each glass. Fill with club soda. Stir once.

PINEAPPLE CREAM SHAKE

½ *cup pineapple juice*   ¼ *cup cream*
1 *scoop soft pineapple*   1 *tablespoon sugar*
sherbet

Beat or blend until foamy. Serve in 1 tall glass.

BLUEBERRY LEMON FLOAT

1 *cup blueberries*   1 *pint lemon sherbet*
½ *cup water*   *Carbonated water*
¼ *cup sugar*

Cook blueberries, water, and sugar in a saucepan 3 to 5 minutes, or until blueberries are soft. Stir occasionally. Strain and chill. Scoop lemon sherbet into 6 glasses. Add blueberry mixture. Fill each glass with carbonated water.

LAVENDER COOLER

½ cup grape juice
1 scoop soft lime sherbet

Beat or blend. Serve in 1 tall glass.

LEMON SPARKLE

¼ cup crushed ice
Juice of ½ lemon
¼ cup grapefruit juice
2 tablespoons blackberry
  syrup

Dash almond extract
  (optional)
1 scoop lemon ice
Tonic or Seven-Up

Put ice into 1 tall glass. Add juices, syrup, and extract. Stir.
Add lemon ice. Fill with Seven-Up or tonic. Stir lightly.

EMERALD ORANGE (B)

Especially thirst-quenching.

⅔ cup pineapple juice
1 scoop orange ice
1 tablespoon mint syrup

2 drops mint extract
Crushed ice
Green maraschino cherry

Blend juice, ice, syrup, mint extract, and crushed ice. Pour
into 1 tall glass. Garnish with cherry.

SYRUP

Children have grown old arguing the meaning and history of egg creams. But one thing is for sure: As the *New York* Magazine of the *Herald Tribune* puts it, in a comprehensive article on the subject, "The true egg cream is something like the Holy Roman Empire in the time of the Habsburgs, being neither holy nor Roman—an egg cream has neither eggs nor cream."

CHOCOLATE EGG CREAM

2 tablespoons chocolate syrup*
2 tablespoons cold milk
Carbonated water

Pour chocolate syrup and milk into 1 soda glass. Fill with carbonated water. Stir lightly.

*CHOCOLATE SYRUP

5 squares bitter chocolate   *Dash salt*
1¼ cups hot water   *¾ teaspoon vanilla*
1¼ cups sugar

Melt chocolate in double boiler. Add hot water, sugar, and salt. Cook 5 minutes, stirring constantly. When mixture is smooth, remove from heat. Let cool. Add vanilla. May be kept in refrigerator in a tightly covered jar. Yields 3 cups.

APRICOT EGG CREAM

2 *tablespoons apricot*   Club soda
  *syrup** *   1 *dried apricot, softened*
2 *tablespoons very cold*   *in water*
  milk

Pour syrup and milk into 1 soda glass. Fill with club soda.
Stir lightly. Garnish with apricot.

*APRICOT SYRUP

  1 *cup sugar*
  2 *cups apricot juice*
  2 *teaspoons lemon juice*

Boil sugar and apricot juice for about 10 minutes. Add lemon
juice. May be kept in refrigerator in a tightly covered jar.
Yields 3 cups.

CHOCOLATE COLA

For teen-agers, when boredom with ordinary chocolate sodas
sets in.

  1 *egg*   Dash cinnamon
  1 *tablespoon chocolate*   Chopped ice
    syrup   Cola

Beat egg well, until lemon-yellow and frothy. Add chocolate
syrup and cinnamon. Beat again. Pour into 4 soda glasses over
chopped ice. Fill with cola. Stir lightly. Serve immediately.

CREAM COLA

Shaved ice   1 tablespoon cream
1½ tablespoons grenadine   Dash cinnamon
Cola

Half fill 1 tall glass with ice. Add grenadine and cola. Stir lightly. Float cream on top. Sprinkle cinnamon on top.

LEMON CREAM SODA

2 tablespoons lemon   Ice cubes
  cream syrup*   Slice of lemon
1 glass Bitter Lemon or
  Seven-Up

Mix syrup in Bitter Lemon or Seven-Up. Pour over ice cubes in 1 tall glass. Stir lightly. Garnish with slice of lemon.

* LEMON CREAM SYRUP (B)

1 peeled lemon, cut up and   1 cup sugar
  seeded   1 pint milk
1 unpeeled lemon, cut up   1 tablespoon lemon extract
  and seeded

Blend lemons and sugar, first on low speed, then on high. When rind is thoroughly grated and sugar is dissolved, add milk and extract. Blend for about 1 minute. May be kept in refrigerator in tightly covered jar.

LEMON SYRUP SODA

Juice of ½ lemon
Scant ¼ cup light corn
  syrup

¼ teaspoon lemon extract
Ice cubes
Club soda

Combine first 3 ingredients to make syrup. Divide into 2 tall glasses. Add ice cubes. Fill glasses with club soda.

CHARTREUSE CHILL

Rich and unusual.

1½ tablespoons lime
  syrup
2 tablespoons orange
  marmalade

1 beaten egg
2 tablespoons cream
  (optional)
Shaved ice

Shake thoroughly. Serve in 1 very tall glass.

PINEAPPLE ALMOND

2 drops almond extract
2 tablespoons pineapple
  syrup*

Small slice of pineapple
Ice cubes
Club soda

Mix extract with syrup. Pour over ice cubes in 1 tall glass. Fill with club soda. Stir lightly. Put pineapple slice on top, with straw through center hole.

*PINEAPPLE SYRUP

¼ cup grated pineapple
½ cup water
½ cup sugar

Bring all ingredients to boiling point. Reduce heat and simmer about 45 minutes. Strain through a wire sieve. May be kept in refrigerator in a tightly covered jar. Yields about 1 cup.

ARBOR COOLER

2 tablespoons pineapple
　syrup
1 tablespoon vanilla syrup
Juice of ½ lime

2 tablespoons grape juice
Cracked ice
Club soda
Wedge of pineapple

Shake all ingredients, except soda and pineapple. Pour mixture into 1 tall glass. Fill with club soda. Stir lightly. Garnish with pineapple wedge.

ORGEAT HIGHBALL

Orgeat is almond-flavored.

⅓ cup orgeat syrup
⅔ cup carbonated water

Crushed ice
Maraschino cherry

Mix syrup, water and ice and pour into 1 tall, cold glass. Garnish with cherry.

ALMOND CREAM FIZZ

3 *tablespoons orgeat syrup*   *Cracked ice*
1 *tablespoon vanilla syrup*   *Carbonated water*
2 *tablespoons cream*

Put first 4 ingredients into 1 tall glass. Fill with carbonated water. Stir lightly.

SWEET COFFEE ALE

2 *tablespoons coffee syrup**   *Cold ginger ale*
2 *tablespoons cold milk*   *Slice of candied ginger*
Ice cubes

Pour syrup and milk over ice cubes in 1 tall glass. Add ginger ale. Stir lightly. Trim rim of glass with ginger.

*COFFEE SYRUP

Use equal parts of very strong coffee and sugar. Simmer 3 minutes. Cool. May be made with instant coffee.

POLAR PASTEL

2 *tablespoons berry syrup*
¾ *cup club soda*
1 *tablespoon sour cream*

Beat or blend. Serve in 1 tall glass.

CHARTS AND TABLES

Herbs and Garnishes

For Ginger Ale and Some Other Standards
　Angostura bitters
　Apple, wedge
　Cherries, fresh
　Cherries, maraschino (green or red)
　Banana, slice
　Cloves
　Cucumber, slice, rind
　Curry (in cola)
　Ginger
　Lemon, slice, spiced slice, rind (curled or grated)
　Mint
　Orange, slice, spiced slice, rind (curled or grated)
　Pineapple, slice, wedge, finger
　Tarragon

For Fruit Juices
　Allspice
　Basil
　Berries
　Brandy extract
　Cherries, fresh
　Cherries, maraschino (red or green)
　Cinnamon, powdered, stick (to use as muddler)
　Cloves, whole (to stick into fruit)
　Fruit, any compatible with drink (stuck with whole spices,
　　fruit swizzle sticks—strung on toothpicks, on kebobs, or
　　on small ornamental skewers)

Jelly, mound (Use color appropriate to drink, do not stir.)
Lemon, slice, spiced slice, rind (curled or grated)
Marjoram
Mint
Nutmeg
Preserves (see Jelly)
Tarragon
Wine, non-alcoholic

For Tomato and Vegetable
Basil
Bay leaves
Carrot, curl, stick
Celery, seed, dried leaves, long stalk in glass
Chervil
Curry
Dill
Kebob (strung with small pieces of raw, mixed vegetables)
Onion powder (scant)
Orégano
Paprika
Parsley
Pepper
Pepper, green
Rosemary
Sage
Sauces, hot (Worcestershire, Tabasco, etc.)
Sour cream, dab
Tarragon
Thyme
Yoghurt, plain (dab)

For Punch
  See *Fruit Juices*
  Gardenias (float in punch bowl)
  Grapes, frozen clusters
  Marshmallows (with milk punch)
  Melon balls
  Sherbet and ices, scoops
  Wreath, leaves made of whole spices with dried berries at-
    tached (around punch bowl at Christmas)

For Coffee
  Angostura bitters
  Brandy extract
  Cardamon
  Chocolate, shaved
  Cinnamon stick (as muddler in hot coffee)
  Coriander
  Lemon, peel
  Mint
  Nuts, chopped
  Orange, peel, rind (grated)
  Rum extract
  Whipped cream

For Tea
  Allspice
  Angostura bitters
  Apple, slice, wedge
  Cinnamon
  Cloves
  Lemon, slice, spiced slice, rind (curled or grated)
  Orange, slice, spiced slice, rind (curled or grated)
  Mint
  Preserves, fruit

For Milk
  Brandy extract
  Chocolate, shaved, bits, syrup
  Cinnamon, powdered, stick
  Marshmallows
  Nutmeg
  Sage (for hot milk)
  Syrups, all flavors

For Fountain Drinks
  Candy bits
  Cherries, maraschino, candied
  Chocolate, shaved, "sprinkles" (or "jimmies")
  Coffee, instant, mixed with sugar (on chocolate or coffee
    drink)
  Fruit, wedges (on rim of glass)
  Marshmallows
  Mint, sprig
  Nuts, chopped
  Whipped cream

OTHER GARNISH IDEAS

CRUSTAS FOR FRUIT DRINKS OR STANDARDS

Cut ends off a lemon or an orange. Cut peel into one long
spiral. Line a wineglass or an old-fashioned glass with the
peel. Wet the edge of the glass with a little water, turn the
glass upside down, and dip the edge into powdered sugar.

ICE CUBES, COLORED

Pour water into ice trays. Add vegetable coloring. Freeze.

ICE CUBES, FLAVORED

Pour fruit juice into ice trays. Freeze.

ICE CUBES, DECORATED

Pour water into ice trays. Add small pieces of fruits or vegetables (depending on drink). Freeze.

FRUIT ICE BLOCKS FOR PUNCHES

I

Line bottom of ice tray with slices of pineapple and maraschino cherries. (Leave divider out.) Pour 2 tablespoons water over fruit. Freeze. Add enough water to just cover fruit. Freeze. Fill tray with water. Freeze. Unmold. Place in punch bowl, fruit-side up.

FRUIT BLOCK

II

Half fill a 1-quart ring mold with fruit juice or soda. Add extra food coloring, if desired. Place in freezer. When partially frozen add a can of fruit cocktail and enough additional juice or soda to fill the ring. Freeze. To unmold, dip bottom of mold in hot water, and remove ice quickly.

GLASSES

To frost, refrigerate. To frost rims, dip edge of glass, first in lemon or orange juice, then into mound of granulated sugar. Chill glass in refrigerator.

In the summer, serve drinks with huge fresh leaves under glasses.

Yields

1 orange: about ⅓ cup juice, about 1 tablespoon rind

1 lemon: about 3 tablespoons juice, about 1½ teaspoons rind

1 lime: about 2 tablespoons juice, about 1½ teaspoons rind

4 ounces almonds, shelled and slivered: approx. ¾ cup

1 trayful ice cubes: 1 quart crushed ice

1 cup cream: 2 cups whipped cream

JUICE YIELDED BY EXTRACTOR (APPROXIMATE)

Apples*	2 medium	1 cup
Banana	1 medium plus	
	1 orange	¾ cup nectar
Beet greens	(from 3 medium beets)	1 cup
Beets	4 medium	1 cup
Cantaloupe	1 ripe	3 cups nectar
Carrots	4 to 5	1 cup
Celery	4 to 5 large stalks	1 cup
Cucumber	1 medium	¾ cup
Grapes, seedless	2 cups (stemmed)	1 cup
Lettuce (romaine)	5 large (outside) leaves	⅓ cup
Onions	3 medium	½ cup
Parsley	stems of 1 large bunch	¼ cup
Peppers, green	2 medium	¼ cup
Pineapple	¼ medium	½ cup
Rhubarb	2 large stalks	½ cup
Spinach	½ pound	⅓ cup
Strawberries	1 cup	½ cup nectar
Watercress	stems of 1 bunch	¼ cup

* To keep juice from turning brown, add a few drops of lemon juice.

Calorie Chart

		Calories
Almonds, shelled	6 medium	50
Apple	2½ inches in diameter	75
Apple cider	1 cup	100
Apple juice	1 cup	125
Apricots	5 medium	100
Apricots, canned or cooked with syrup	3 halves	50
Avocado	½ small	125
Banana	1 medium	100
Beef, chopped	¼ pound	325
Beef broth	1 cup	35
Beets	½ cup	35
Blackberries, canned	1 cup	200
Blackberries, fresh	1 cup	100
Blueberries, canned	½ cup	125
Blueberries, fresh	1 cup	100
Borscht, plain	1 cup	75
Bouillon	1 cup	25
Buttermilk	1 cup	85
Cabbage, raw	¾ cup	20
Cantaloupe	½ medium	40
Carbonated fruit drinks	average glass	75
Carrot	1 medium	25
Carrot juice	1 cup	50
Celery, raw	2 stalks	10
Cherries, canned	20 small	75
Cherries, fresh	25 small	75
Chocolate bar	average	250
Chocolate milk	1 cup	225
Chocolate syrup	1 tablespoon	50
Chocolate syrup, dietetic	1 tablespoon	about 9
Cider	1 cup scant	100

		Calories
Citron, candied	1 ounce	100
Clam juice	6 ounces	50
Cocoa, powdered	1½ tablespoons	50
Cocoa, with milk	1 cup	225
Coconut, dried	2 tablespoons	50
Coconut, fresh	1 slice, 2×1×½ inches	100
Coffee, black		0
Cola	6 ounces	75
Consommé	1 cup	25
Corn oil	1 tablespoon	100
Corn syrup	2 tablespoons	125
Cranberry juice cocktail	1 cup	105
Cream, light	3 tablespoons	100
Cream, medium	2½ tablespoons	100
Cream, heavy, whipping	1 tablespoon	50
Cream, whipped	1 tablespoon	33
Cream, whipped, low calorie	1 tablespoon	3
Cucumber	1 8-inch	20
Dandelion greens	½ cup	50
Dates, fresh and dried	1 cup	505
Egg	1 average	75
Eggnog, average	1 cup	300
Egg white	1	15
Egg yolk	1	60
Figs, fresh	4 large	50
Ginger ale	6 ounces	75
Grapefruit	½ small	50
Grapefruit, canned	½ cup	75
Grapefruit juice, frozen concentrate	6-ounce can	350
Grapefruit juice, frozen concentrate, water added	1 cup	100
Grapefruit juice, sweetened	6 ounces	75
Grape juice	1 cup	150
Grape juice, frozen concentrate, unsweetened	6-ounce can	300

Calories

Grape juice, frozen		
concentrate, water added	1 cup	100
Grapes, Concord	30 average	100
Honey	1 tablespoon	65
Honeydew melon	¼ average	65
Ice cream (vanilla)	⅙ quart (1 large scoop)	185
Ice cream soda	1 average	350
Ice milk (vanilla)	⅙ quart (1 large scoop)	135
Ices	½ cup	150
Jams, marmalades,		
preserves	1 tablespoon	55
Lemon	1 medium	25
Lemonade	1 cup	100
Lemonade, frozen		
concentrate, unsweetened	6-ounce can	430
Lemonade, frozen		
concentrate, water added	1 cup	110
Lemon juice	½ cup	30
Lemon-lime drink	12 ounces	150
Lemon soda	6 ounces	75
Lettuce	¼ head	10
Lime	1 medium	20
Limeade, frozen		
concentrate, sweetened	1 cup	405
Limeade, frozen		
concentrate, water added	1 cup	105
Lime juice	1 cup	60
Loganberries, canned	½ cup	50
Loganberries, fresh	⅔ cup	50
Loganberry juice	6 ounces	75
Malted milk, average	1 portion	400
Mango	1 average	100
Maple syrup	1 tablespoon	50
Marshmallow	1 average	25
Marshmallows	1 ounce	90
Milk	1 cup	157
Milk, condensed	1 tablespoon	50

		Calories
Milk, evaporated	¼ cup	50
Milk, skim	1 cup	80
Milk shake	1	350
Mint jelly, low calorie	1 tablespoon	2
Molasses	1 tablespoon	50
Olives	6 small	50
Orange	1 medium	75
Orange juice, fresh	6 ounces	75
Orange juice, frozen concentrate	6-ounce can	330
Orange juice, frozen concentrate, water added	1 cup	110
Ovaltine	1 cup	150
Parsley	1 tablespoon	2
Papaya, raw	½-inch cubes, 1 cup	70
Peach, canned	2 halves	75
Peach, fresh	1 medium	50
Peach nectar, canned	1 cup	115
Pear, fresh	1 medium	75
Pear nectar	1 cup	130
Persimmon	1 medium	100
Pineapple, canned	1 slice	75
Pineapple, fresh	1 cup	75
Pineapple juice, canned	1 cup	125
Pistachio nuts	8	25
Plums, canned	2 medium	75
Plums, fresh	2	50
Pomegranate	1 average	100
Prune juice	6 ounces	200
Prunes, cooked	3	100
Prunes, dried	4	100
Raisins, seeded	½ cup	225
Raspberries, canned	½ cup	100
Raspberries, fresh	½ cup	50
Rhubarb, stewed (no sugar)	1 cup	35
Root beer soda	6 ounces	75
Sherbet	½ cup	200

		Calories
Sour cream	¼ cup	200
Strawberries, cooked or canned	1 cup	225
Strawberries, fresh	1 cup	50
Strawberries, frozen	10-ounce carton	300
Sugar, brown	1 tablespoon	40
Sugar, powdered	1 tablespoon	30
Sugar, white	1 teaspoon	20
Syrup (see Chocolate syrup)		
Tangerine	1 large	35
Tea, plain		0
Tomato, fresh	1 medium	25
Tomato juice	1 cup	50
Vegetable juice	6 ounces	75
Walnuts	4	100
Watermelon	1 medium slice	100
Yoghurt, plain	1 cup	130
Yoghurt, vanilla	1 cup	165
Yoghurt, with fruit preserves	1 cup	260

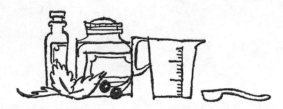

INDEX

Ades, 38–40
  agua de melao, 40
  defined, 38
  golden lemonade, 39–40
  kumquat-lime, 39
  lemonade (basic), 38
  lemon-orange, 39
  lime-lemon, 39
  lime-orange, 39
  pink lemonade, 39
  spiced lemonade, 40
Adults only, 63
After-dinner drinks, 103 ff
Agua de melao, 40
Alcoholic drink: percentage of alcohol, 79
Alexander, almost, 85
Alfalfa leaf tea, 125
Alfalfa mint tea, 125
All-day diet, 148
Almond: cream fizz, 179
  drink, Spanish, 77
  flip, 147
  foam, 147
Almondine coffee, 111
Almost alexander, 85
Anise milk, 137
Anise tea, 123
Apple: cocktail, red, 84
  cream, 169
  juice, 50–52
    apricot, 50
    autumn, 51
    entrées after, 50
    prune, 51
    summer, 50–51
    winelike, 84
  surprise, 52, 84

Apples, juice yield, 193
Après school cocktail, 146
Apricot: apple, 50
  buttermilk breeze, 155
  capricot, 67
  cream coffee, 115
  egg cream, 175
  mint ice cream soda, 163
  nog, 150
  syrup, 175
  tea punch, 129
Arbor cooler, 178
Arrack: coffee grog, 87
  mock, 86
  Scotch Irish coffee, 87
  Tahitian tingle, 86–87
Assam tea, 120
Autumn apple, 51

(B) defined, 15
Banana: cream, 167
  foam, 44
  juice yield, 193
  nog, 150
  whip, 144
  yoghurt swirl, 159
B and T in a cup, 62
Basket-fired tea, 120
Bavarian tomato cocktail, 61
"Beat" defined, 16
Beet(s): borscht belt, 65
  juice yield, 193
  treat, 68
Bengal broth, 76
Bitter lemon, 29, 31–33
  lemonescence, 45
  pineapple mint, 45
Bitters and iced coffee, 115

Black and white ice cream soda, 163
Black teas, 120
"Blend" defined, 16
Blender breakfast, 153
Blueberry lemon float, 172
Blue punch, 99–100
Bogus booze, 79–89
  almost alexander, 85
  arrack, mock, 86
  bride's bowl, 83
  café brûlot, 88
  cherri julep, 85
  cherry rickey, 86
  coffee grog, 87
  cucumber wine punch, 81
  ginger beer, 88
  "liqueurs" or "cordials," 85–89
  mock bishop, 82–83
  mock champagne cocktail, 83
  mock whiskey eggnog, 88
  mock wine cup, 81
  negus, 82
  non-alcoholic crème de menthe
    frappé, 86
  non-rose cocktail, 82
  phony island rum, 89
  red apple cocktail, 84
  Scotch Irish coffee, 87
  Tahitian tingle, 86–87
Bombay cooler, 160
Borscht belt, 65
Bride's bowl, 83
Broth, Bengal, 76
Buttermilk, 155–58
  apricot breeze, 155
  brunch, 156
  cherry fizz, 158
  farmer's market, 157
  fruit whirl, 156–57
  pineapple, 155–56
  spice apple, 156
  strawberry, 155
  vanilla fizz, 157

Café au lait, 109
Café brûlot, 88
Calcutta cola, 33
California cider, 133
Calorie chart, 195–99
Camomile tea, 125
Cape Cod tea punch, 129

Capricot, 67
Carbonated water, club soda, 16
Cardamon coffee, 118
Caribbean cocktail, 25
Carrot(s): Dutch dream, 61
  grapefruit cocktail, 67
  juice yield, 193
  milk blend, 145
Ceylon tea, 120
Champagne cocktail, mock, 83
Chartreuse chill, 177
Cherri julep, 85
Cherry: buttermilk fizz, 158
  chocolate for children, 140
  nut ice cream soda, 164
  papaya cream whip, 54
  papaya mix, 54
  pink, 41–42
  rickey, 86
Children's custard drink, 138
Chocolate: cherry, for children, 140
  chip coffee ice cream soda, 163
  cola, 175
  egg cream, 174
  excelsior, hot, 140
  hot: easy, 139
    Mexican, 141
  milk: cinnamon, 146
    St. Thomas, 145
  syrup, 174
Christmas drink, Dutch, 138
Church punch for 100, 101–2
Cider: California, 133
  eggnog, 149
  hot mulled, 132–33
  rickey, 22
Cinnamon chocolate, 146
Citrus cream, 168
Clam juice: adults only, 63
  marina cocktail, 63
  pink clam cocktail, 62
  tomato clam blend, 62
Clam yoghurt cocktail, 160
Club soda: carbonated water, 16
  cocktails, 29–35
  pink drink, 33
Cocktails: bogus booze, 79–89
  club sodas, 29–35
  colas, 29–35
  extracts, essences, etc., 69–77

fruit juice-vegetable juice mixed,
    65–68
gingerale, 19–27
juices: fruit and vegetable, 37–68
other standards, 29–35
punch, 91–102
soup, 75–76
tonics, 29–35
vegetable juice, 58–65
Cocoa, hot, 139
Coffee, 105–18
    almondine, 111
    apricot cream, 115
    bitters and iced, 115
    café au lait, 109
    café brûlot, 88
    cappuccino, 108
    cardamon, 118
    chocolaccino, 110
    cola, 117
    cold, 113–18
    creole, 112
    dietetic mocha froth, 114
    drip method, 107
    espresso, 108
    for fifty, 107
    frosted Hawaii, 116
    froth, 114
    grog, 87
    herbs and garnishes, 185
    hot, 106–12
    hot mocha froth, 110–11
    hot mocha java, 109
    ice and spice, 117
    ice cube, 113
    iced, 113
        and bitters, 115
        espresso, 114
    instant iced: for one, 113
        for fifty, 113
    kahului, 110
    maple coffee ice, 116
    mid-Eastern, 112
    mocha frost, 114–15
    nectar, 117
    Pennsylvania mocha, 116
    percolator method, 106
    pink and white dessert, 112
    Scotch Irish, 87
    syrup, 179
    tonic, 30
    Turkish, 111
    vacuum method, 107
    Viennese, 109
Cola cocktails, 29–35
    Calcutta cola, 33
    lemon-egg cola, 34
    mint cola, 34
Cola coffee, 117
Cold coffee, 113–18
Coney Island ice cream soda, 164
Coney Island root beer, 34
"Cordials." See "Liqueurs" or "Cor-
    dials"
Cranberry: cream, 53
    lime cooler, 52
    nog, 150
    pastel pink, 53
Cream cola, 176
Crème de menthe frappé, non-alco-
    holic, 86
Creole coffee, 112
Crushed ice: in blender, 11
    blended with drink, 16
Crustas, 186
Cucumber: cream, 64
    juice yield, 193
    wine punch, 81
"Cup" defined, 16
Currant: cream cooler, 167
    punch, holiday, 100–1
Custard drink, children's, 138

(D) defined, 15
Daiquiris (blender), 46–47
Darjeeling tea, 120
Definitions and explanations, 15–16
Desert herb tea, 125
Diet drinks, 15
Dieter's instant ice cream soda, 162
Dietetic mocha froth, 114
Dixie almond, 138–39
Drinks, after and before dinner: cof-
    fee, 105–18
    fountain, 161–80
    hot shots, 131–42
    mostly milk, 143–60
    tea, 119–30
Dr. Pepper, hot, 133
Dutch: Christmas drink, 138
    dream, 61

mocha, 141
sage milk, 137

Earl Grey tea, 120
Easy hot chocolate, 139
Eggnogs, 148–50
  apricot, 150
  banana, 150
  cider, 149
  cranberry, 150
  holiday, 149
  lime, 154
  mock whiskey, 88
  simple, 148–49
  vita, 154
Emerald orange, 173
English: breakfast tea, 120
  holiday hot tea punch, 124
Equipment, 11–13
Equivalents, table, 191
Espresso coffee, 108
  iced, 114
Essences. See Extracts, essences, etc.
Extracts, 79
  arrack, mock, 86
  mock, 88
  See also Extracts, essences, etc.
Extracts, essences, etc., 69–77
  Bengal broth, 76
  coconut tropical, 77
  herb sour, 70
  Jaipur ginger, 72–73
  jumping juniper, 71
  orange-blossom water afshoreh, 74
  Persian mint drink, 72
  rose drink, 73–74
  rosemary, 71
  rose or orange-blossom water af-
    shoreh, 74
  saffron cocktail, 70
  slow soup fizz, 75
  soup and soda, 75
  Spanish almond drink, 77
  Tarzan dinner drink, 76
  violet afshoreh, 74

Farmer's market, 157
Farm froth, 38, 66–67
Fennel seed tea, 125
Fenugreek seed tea, 125
Finnish punch bowl, 97

Float, 165
Flower-essence drinks, 69
  orange-blossom water afshoreh, 74
  rose drink, 73–74
  rose-water afshoreh, 74
  violet afshoreh, 74
Formosa oolong tea, 121
Fountain drinks, 161–80
  dieter's instant ice cream soda, 162
  ice cream soda, 162
  ice cream soda and combinations,
    163–73 (see also under name)
  sherbets and ices, 169–73
  syrup, 174–80
Fresh peach ice cream soda, 164
Frosted, 165
Frosted coffee Hawaii, 116
Frosting glasses, 188
Fruit: bowl, 43
  cream (see Banana cream)
  drinks: crustas, 186
    hot, 132
  fizz punch, 93
  float, 170
  frappé, 145
  ice blocks, for punch, 187–88
  juice yield, 193
  milk, 144
  punch: hot Finnish, 135
    sparkling, 95
  sherbet punch, 96
  tea: hot, 124
    swizzle, 128
  whirl, buttermilk, 156–57
  yoghurt, 158
Fruit juice cocktails, 37–68
  ades, 38–40
  apple juice, 50–52
  apple surprise, 52
  apricot apple, 50
  autumn apple, 51
  banana foam, 44
  cherry papaya cream whip, 54
  cherry papaya mix, 54
  cherry pink, 41–42
  cranberry cream, 53
  cranberry lime cooler, 52
  fruit bowl, 43
  gin-less gimlet, 41
  girl talk, 57
  grape cocktail, 57

grapefruit ginger, 49
Haitian splash, 55
herbed fruit, 45
herbs and garnishes, 183–84
honey grape drink, 43
instant Waikiki, 40
island mist, 48
juice julep, 38, 48
lavender-lemon highball, 43
lemonescence, 45
lime daiquiri, 46
melon cocktail, 54–55
mint apricot, 49
morning cocktail, 41
neat peach, 58
1920 cocktail, 42
orange daiquiri, 47
orange frost, 47
pale citron, 50
Palm Beach cocktail, 42
papaya cherry cream whip, 54
papaya cherry mix, 54
pastel pink, 54
pineapple daiquiri, 47
pineapple froth, 44
pineapple mint, 45
pineapple pink, 46
pink peach, 57
pink rhubarb, 56
pink sands, 44
prune apple, 51
rose whirl, 55
strawberry crush, 56
summer apple, 50–51
-vegetable juice cocktails, 65–68
white grape cocktail, 56
Fruit juice and vegetable juice mixed,
    65–68
  beet treat, 68
  capricot, 67
  farm froth, 66–67
  grapefruit carrot cocktail, 67
  pineapple parsnip, 65
  pineapple protein plus, 66
  sangrita, 65
  vegetable fruit blend, 66

Garden appetizer, 64
Garnishes: crustas, 186
  for glasses, 188

ice cubes: colored, 187
  decorated, 187
  flavored, 187
  See also Herbs and garnishes
Ginger ale, herbs and garnishes, 183
Ginger ale cocktails, 19–27
  advantages, 19
  Caribbean cocktail, 25
  cider rickey, 22
  ginger froth, 23
  gingerparilla, 23
  herb sizzle, 26
  and juice, 20–21
  lemon froth, 22
  mint mist, 25
  mixed fruit thaw, 26
  peach thaw, 27
  pony's neck, 22
  prohibition spice, 24–25
  Shirley Temple Sardi, 21
  tall clove purple, 24
  white grape nectar, 23
Ginger: beer, 88
  froth, 23
  Indonesian, 134–35
  Jaipur, 72–73
  mist, 170
  smoothie, 169
  syrup, 73
Gingerparilla, 23
Gin-less gimlet, 41
Girl talk, 57
"Glass": defined, 16
  "juice," 16
  "small," 16
  "soda," 16
  "tall," 16
  "very tall," 16
Golden lemonade, 39–40
Graduation punch, 97
Grand illusion, 151
Grape(s): cocktail, 57
  girl talk, 57
  honey, drink, 43
  juice julep, 48
  juice yield, 193
  lavender-lemon highball, 43
  1920 cocktail, 42
  white, cocktail, 56
Grapefruit: carrot cocktail, 67
  fruit bowl, 43

ginger, 49
mint apricot, 49
Green garden cocktail, 63
Green teas, 120
Gunpowder tea, 120

Haitian splash, 55
Hawaiian milk shake, 152
Herb: cream tomato juice, 60
  drinks (see Herb drinks)
  sizzle, 26
  sour, 70
  teas, 125
Herb drinks, 69
  herb sour, 70
  Jaipur ginger, 72-73
  jumping juniper, 71
  Persian mint drink, 72
  rosemary, 71
  saffron cocktail, 70
Herbed fruit, 45
Herbs and garnishes, 183-86
  for coffee, 185
  fountain drinks, 186
  fruit juices, 183-84
  ginger ale and other standards, 183
  milk, 186
  punch, 185
  tea, 185
  tomato and vegetable, 184
Hoboken ice cream soda, 163
Holiday currant punch, 100-1
Holiday eggnog, 149
Honey grape drink, 43
Horchata de almendras (Spanish al-
    mond drink), 77
Hot chocolate: easy, 139
  excelsior, 140
  Mexican, 141
Hot: cocoa, 139
  coffee, 106-10
  Dr. Pepper, 133
  Finnish fruit punch, 135
  fruit drink, 132
  fruit tea, 124
  Jamaica punch, 137
  lemon tea, 122
  mocha java, 109
  molasses and milk, 142

mulled cider, 132-33
shots, 131-42
tea, 121-25

Ice and spice coffee, 117
Ice cream punch, 101
Ice cream soda, 162
Ice cream soda combinations: apple
    cream, 169
  apricot mint, 163
  banana cream, 167
  black and white, 163
  cherry nut, 164
  chocolate chip coffee, 163
  citrus cream, 168
  Coney Island, 164
  currant cream cooler, 167
  float, 165
  fresh peach, 164
  frosted, 165
  fruit cream (see Banana cream)
  ginger smoothie, 169
  Hoboken, 163
  malted milk, 163
  maple fizz, 166-67
  melon cream shake, 168
  milk shake, 165
  mocha froth, 166
  peaches-and-cream frosted, 168
  Viennese velvet, 166
Ice cube coffee, 113
Ice cubes: colored, 187
  decorated, 187
  flavored, 187
Iced Coffee, 113
  bitters and, 115
  espresso, 114
Iced tea, 126
  for one, 126
  for fifty, 126
  instant, 127
  lemonade, 127
  lemon frosted, 127-28
  strawberry fizz, 128
Indonesian ginger, 134-35
Instant iced coffee: for one, 113
  for fifty, 113
Instant iced tea, 127
Instant Waikiki, 40
Island mist, 48

Jaipur ginger, 72–73
Jamaica punch, hot, 137
Jasmine tea, 121
(JE) defined, 15
Juice: and ginger ale, 20–21
  "glass," defined, 16
  julep, 38, 48
  yields, 193
Juices: defined, 37
  fruit (*see* Fruit *and* Fruit juice cocktails)
  fruit and vegetable cocktails, 37–68
  vegetable (*see* Vegetable juice cocktails)
Jumping juniper, 71
Juniper, jumping, 71

Keemun tea, 120
Kumquat-limeade, 39

Lapsang souchong tea, 120
Lavender cooler, 173
Lavender-lemon highball, 43
Lemon: cream soda, 176
  cream syrup, 176
  -egg cola, 34
  frosted iced tea, 127–28
  froth, 22
  juice yield, 193
  -lavender highball, 43
  -orangeade, 39
  orange fizz, 171
  sparkle, 173
  syrup soda, 177
  tea, hot, 122
  See also Bitter lemon *and* Lemonade
Lemonade (basic), 38
  golden, 39–40
  pink, 39
  spiced, 40
Lemonescence, 45
Lime: blossom tea, 125
  daiquiri, 46
  eggnog, 154
  gin-less gimlet, 41
  juice yield, 193
  -lemonade, 39
  -orangeade, 39
Lindenblüten tea, 125

"Liqueurs" or "cordials," 85–89
  almost alexander, 85
  arrack, 86
  café brûlot, 88
  cherri julep, 85
  cherry rickey, 86
  coffee grog, 87
  ginger beer, 88
  mock whiskey eggnog, 88
  non-alcoholic crème de menthe frappé, 86
  phony island rum, 89
  Scotch Irish coffee, 87
  Tahitian tingle, 86–87

Malted milk, 165
Maple coffee ice, 116
Maple fizz, 166–67
Marina cocktail, 63
Maté tea, 125
Melon: cocktail, 54–55
  cream shake, 168
  punch bowl, 98
Mexican fruit punch, 96–97
Mexican hot chocolate, 141
Michigan gubernatorial punch, 92
Mid-Eastern coffee, 112
Milk, 143–60
  all-day diet, 148
  almond flip, 147
  almond foam, 147
  anise, 137
  après school cocktail, 146
  apricot nog, 150
  banana nog, 150
  banana whip, 144
  blender breakfast, 153
  buttermilk, 155–58
  carrot milk blend, 145
  cider eggnog, 149
  cinnamon chocolate, 146
  cranberry nog, 150
  drinks, 143–60
  Dutch sage, 137
  eggnogs, 148–50
  fruit frappé, 145
  fruit milk, 144
  grand illusion, 151
  Hawaiian milk shake, 152
  herbs and garnishes, 186
  holiday eggnog, 149

lime eggnog, 154
malted, 165
orange, 152
peach, 152
peanut butter, 146–47
St. Thomas chocolate, 145
shake, 165
  Hawaiian, 152
simple eggnog, 148–49
skim, 151–54
strawberry rennet drink, 153
vegetable, 148
vita eggnog, 154
yoghurt, 158–60
See also Buttermilk *and* Yoghurt
Mint: apricot, 49
  cola, 34
  drink, Persian, 72
  mist, 25
Mixed fruit thaw, 26
Mocha, Dutch, 141
  frost, 114–15
  froth, 166
    dietetic, 114
    hot, 110–11
  java, hot, 109
  Pennsylvania, 116
Mock: bishop, 82–83
  champagne cocktail, 83
  whiskey eggnog, 88
  wine cup, 81
Molasses and milk, hot, 142
Morning cocktail, 41
Moroccan tea, 122–23

Neat peach, 58
Nectar frost, 171
Negus, 82
1920 cocktail, 42
Non-alcoholic crème de menthe
  frappé, 86
Non-alcoholic drink, defined, 15
Non-bloody Mary, 58
Non-drinker's drink, defined, 15
Non-rose cocktail, 82

Oolong tea, 121
Orange: -blossom water afshoreh, 74
  cherry pink, 41–42
  daiquiri, 47
  freeze, 169

freeze float, 170
frost, 47
island mist, 48
juice yield, 193
-lemonade, 39
-limeade, 39
milk, 152
morning cocktail, 41
pale citron, 50
Palm Beach cocktail, 42
punch, White House, 92
sangrita, 65
Orgeat highball, 178
Other standard cocktails, 29–35
  bitter lemon, 31–33
  Calcutta cola, 33
  coffee tonic, 30
  Coney Island root beer, 34
  herbs and garnishes, 183
  lemon-egg cola, 34
  mint cola, 34
  pink drink, 33
  seventeen, 35
  tea tonic, 31
  tonic drink, 30

Pale citron, 50
Palm Beach cocktail, 42
Papaya cherry: cream whip, 54
  mix, 54
Parsnip, pineapple, 65
Party punch, 94–95
Pastel pink, 53
Peaches(es): -and-cream frosted, 168
  ice cream soda, fresh, 164
  milk, 152
  neat, 58
  pink, 57
  thaw, 27
Peanut butter milk, 146–47
Pennsylvania mocha, 116
Pep in a glass, 64
Peppermint tea, 125
Persian mint drink, 72
Phony island rum, 89
Pineapple: almond, 177
  buttermilk, 155–56
  cream shake, 172
  daiquiri, 47
  froth, 44
  instant Waikiki, 40

juice yield, 193
mint, 45
parsnip, 65
pink, 46
pink sands, 44
protein plus, 66
syrup, 178
Pink: and white dessert coffee, 112
  clam cocktail, 62
  drink, 33
  honey punch, 94
  lemonade, 39,
  peach, 57
  rhubarb, 56
  sands, 44
Polar pastel, 180
Pony's neck, 22
Prohibition spice, 24–25
Prom punch, 93
Prune apple, 51
Punch, 91–102
  apricot tea, 129
  blue, 99–100
  bride's bowl, 83
  Cape Cod tea, 129
  church, for 100, 101–2
  cucumber wine, 81
  "cup," defined, 16
  English holiday hot tea, 124
  Finnish bowl, 97
  fruit fizz, 93
  fruit ice block for, 187–88
  fruit sherbet, 96
  graduation, 97
  herbs and garnishes, 185
  hot Finnish fruit, 135
  hot Jamaica, 137
  holiday currant, 100–1
  ice cream, 101
  melon bowl, 98
  Mexican fruit, 96–97
  Michigan gubernatorial, 92
  mock whiskey eggnog, 88
  party, 94–95
  pink honey, 94
  prom, 93
  rhubarb, 98
  sparkling fruit, 95
  terrace, 96
  Waikiki, 130

watermelon froth, 99
White House orange, 92
Pungent hot tea, 122

Raspberries, Russian, 136
Raspberry: lemonade, 171–72
  soda yoghurt, 159
Red: apple cocktail, 84
  clover tea, 125
Rhubarb: juice yield, 193
  pink, 56
  punch, 98
Root beer: Coney Island, 35
  seventeen, 35
Rose: drink, 73–74
  hip tea, 125
  or orange-blossom water afshoreh,
    74
  syrup, 74
  whirl, 55
Rosemary, 71
Rum, phony island, 89
Russian: holiday tea, 123
  raspberries, 136
  tea, 123

Saffron cocktail, 70
St. Thomas chocolate, 145
Sangrita, 65
Sauerkraut: Bavarian tomato cock-
    tail, 61
  cocktail, 61
  Dutch dream, 61
Scotch Irish coffee, 87
Seventeen, 35
"Shake," defined, 16
Shavegrass tea, 125
Sherbet and ices: blueberry lemon
    float, 172
  emerald orange, 173
  fruit float, 170
  ginger mist, 170
  lavender cooler, 173
  lemon orange fizz, 171
  lemon sparkle, 173
  nectar frost, 171
  orange freeze, 169
  orange freeze float, 170
  pineapple cream shake, 172
  raspberry lemonade, 171–72
Shirley Temple Sardi, 21

Simple eggnog, 148–49
Skim milk, 151–54
  blender breakfast, 153
  grand illusion, 151
  Hawaiian milk shake, 152
  lime eggnog, 154
  orange, 152
  peach, 152
  strawberry rennet drink, 153
  vita eggnog, 154
Slow soup fizz, 75
"Small glass," defined, 16
"Snow" defined, 16
"Soda glass," defined, 16
Soup, 75–76
  and soda, 75
  Bengal broth, 76
  slow fizz, 75
  tartar's tea, 134
  Tarzan dinner drink, 76
Spanish almond drink, 77
Sparkling fruit punch, 95
Spice: and ice coffee, 117
  apple buttermilk, 156
Spiced: lemonade, 40
  sugar syrup, 42
Strawberry: buttermilk, 155
  crush, 56
  iced tea fizz, 128
  juice yield, 193
  rennet drink, 153
Sumatra tea, 120
Summer apple, 50–51
Sweet coffee ale, 179
Syrian drink, 135
Syrups: almond cream fizz, 179
  apricot, 175
  apricot egg dream, 175
  arbor cooler, 178
  chartreuse chill, 177
  chocolate, 174
  chocolate cola, 175
  chocolate egg cream, 174
  coffee, 179
  cream cola, 176
  ginger, 73
  lemon cream, 176
  lemon cream soda, 176
  lemon soda, 177
  orgeat highball, 178
  pineapple, 178

  pineapple almond, 177
  polar pastel, 180
  rose, 74
  sweet coffee ale, 179

Tables: calorie chart, 195–99
  equivalents, 191
  juice yield, 193
  weights and measures, 189
Tahitian tingle, 86–87
Tall clove purple, 24
Tartar's tea, 134
Tarzan dinner drink, 76
Tea, 119–30
  alfalfa leaf, 125
  alfalfa mint, 125
  anise, 123
  apricot punch, 129
  assam, 120
  basket-fired, 120
  black, 120
  camomile, 125
  Cape Cod punch, 129
  Ceylon, 120
  cold, 126–30
  concentrate, 121
  Darjeeling, 120
  desert herb, 125
  Earl Grey, 120
  English breakfast, 120
  English holiday hot punch, 124
  fennel seed, 125
  fenugreek seed, 125
  Formosa oolong, 121
  fruit-, swizzle, 128
  green, 120
  gunpowder, 120
  herb, 125
  herbs and garnishes, 185
  hot, 121–25
  hot fruit, 124
  hot lemon, 122
  iced, 126
    for one, 126
    for fifty, 126
  iced lemonade, 127
  instant iced, 127
  jasmine, 121
  Keemun, 120
  Lapsang souchong, 120
  lemon frosted iced, 127–28

Lindenblüten (lime blossom), 125
maté, 125
Moroccan, 122–23
oolong, 121
peppermint, 125
pungent hot, 122
red clover, 125
rose hip, 125
Russian, 123
Russian holiday, 123
shavegrass, 125
strawberry iced tea fizz, 128
Sumatra, 120
tisane for one, 125
tisanes, 125
tonic, 31
Waikiki punch, 130
Terrace punch, 96
Tisane(s), 125
for one, 125
Tomato juice: B and T in a cup, 62
Bavarian cocktail, 61
clam blend, 62
cocktail, 59
herb cream, 60
herbs and garnishes, 184
non-bloody Mary, 58
sangrita, 65
sauerkraut cocktail, 61
Tonic: cocktails, 29–35
coffee, 30
drink, 30
tea, 31
Turkish coffee, 111

Vanilla buttermilk fizz, 157
Vegetable: milk, 148
juice (see Fruit juice and vegetable
juice mixed)
tomato cocktail, 59
Vegetable juice cocktails, 37–68
adults only, 63
B and T in a cup, 62
Bavarian tomato, 61
borscht belt, 65
cucumber cream, 64

Dutch dream, 61
farm froth, 38
fruit blend, 66
garden appetizer, 64
green garden, 63
herb cream tomato juice, 60
marina cocktail, 63
non-bloody Mary, 58
pep in a glass, 64
pink clam cocktail, 62
sauerkraut cocktail, 61
tomato clam blend, 62
tomato juice, 59
vegetable tomato, 59
Vegetables: herbs and garnishes, 184
juice yield, 193
Vegetarian liquid luncheon, 159
Viennese coffee, 109
Viennese velvet, 160
Violet afshoreh, 74
Vita eggnog, 154

Waikiki punch, 130
Watermelon froth punch, 99
Weights and measures, table, 189
Whiskey eggnog, mock, 88
White grape cocktail, 56
White grape nectar, 23
White House orange punch, 92
Wines, pseudo, 80–81
bride's bowl, 83
cucumber wine punch, 81
mock bishop, 82–83
mock champagne cocktail, 83
mock wine cup, 81
negus, 82
non-rose cocktail, 82
red apple cocktail, 84

Yoghurt, 158–60
banana swirl, 159
Bombay cooler, 160
clam cocktail, 160
fruit, 158
raspberry soda, 159
vegetarian liquid luncheon, 159

g